A Delightful Treasure

Christian Stories for Children and the Adults Who Love Them

by

Shirley McCoy

A Delightful Treasure

Christian Stories for Children and the Adults Who Love Them

ISBN: 978-1-953114-36-5

Illustration credits on Page 148

Photo credits:
Photo of author's original song, name, is taken from author's personal files.

Cover Illustration:
Cover Design: Bob Ousnamer

Published by EA Books Publishing a division of
Living Parables of Central Florida, Inc. a 501c3
EABooksPublishing.com

EABooks Publishing
Your Partner In Publishing

Table of Contents

Part 4 — POETRY AND MUSIC

Part 5 — HIDDEN TREASURE

Acknowledgements

First John 4:19 says "we love because he first loved us" (NAS). God's love has filled the hearts of so many people to help make this book possible. Certainly, my parental family laid a loving Christian foundation. And teachers at church (and in the era in which I grew up, also at public schools) both taught and lived godly lives, for which I gave — and still give — thanks.

I have four wonderful, married children, all encouraging and wonderfully supportive in any way you can think of — and likely beyond. Their/my brood is constantly growing. I believe all children's births are miracles in God's eyes but the facts of some of my families' infants' birthing processes and survivals through early childhood are miracles by anyone's definition. Another answer to prayers and applicable as proof that "we love because He first loved us."

Finally, and actually foremost, my acknowledgement is of the awesome love God shows to His entire creation. How wonderfully blessed we are to be known and so tremendously loved by our heavenly Father, His coming-again Son who gave His life to bring us all into His family, and the Holy Spirit, who speaks to us through scripture and His whisper in/to our minds and hearts. A firm yet gentle reminder that we truly love God *because He first loved us*.

A Delightful Treasure

Christian Stories for Children and the Adults Who Love Them

by

Shirley McCoy

Part 1 —GETTING STARTED

Hi! I'm Shirley McCoy, the person who wrote all the stories in this book. If I could see you I'd give you a big smile; and if you like hugs like I do we could share a hug. But if you're not the hugging type I might ask you where you live. Or if you have a pet. Or what your favorite song or book is. That way we could begin to get to know each other.

Since we can't see each other I hope these first four stories help you feel like we're getting well enough acquainted that you'll eagerly look forward to all that lies ahead.

WE ACCEPTED CHRIST ON A 30-DAY TRIAL

The warm evening air gently caressed us as we strolled hand-in-hand along the gravelly country road fronting our ten-acre farm. What an idyllic setting! The sunrises and sunsets had thrilled my husband Bob and me from the day we moved into this solid, old farmhouse a few months earlier. And a local young woman's two horses grazing in our fields only made it more picturesque. With thirty-some years of our lives behind us, we planned to live out our days there, raising our children and foster children the rest of our lives. But God had other, better plans for us.

As pleased as we were with our rural setting, we still felt something was missing in our lives. We couldn't have been more content with our marriage of three-and-a-half years. Bob had accepted my children from a prior marriage as though they were his own, and then the two of us had been blessed with a son. Yet the "something missing" kept niggling around the edges of our otherwise ideal lives.

Thankfully, God was not unaware of our yearning, and He began to marvelously arrange for our path to intersect with Him. Our nearest neighbors paid us a visit, inviting us to church. "Could this be what's missing?" we wondered, and we attended services with them.

Almost simultaneously, a stranger appeared at our door about seven o'clock one evening, introducing himself as "Pastor John," the father of the young woman who kept her horses on our farm. We invited him in and, after small talk, listened attentively as he tried to show us from scripture that we were sinners and needed Christ as our Savior.

We were almost insulted! We had both been raised in the church and were good people who didn't break the Commandments! But Pastor John's knowledge of God's Word, and his sincerity, love and wisdom really impressed us. At three in the morning, with us still unconvinced that we were sinners, he concluded his visit by presenting us with a challenge:

"Begin reading the Bible daily, praying, and attending church. After 30 days if you don't believe Christ is who He claimed to be, I won't push you to make a commitment to Him." He even said he didn't care whether we went to the church he pastored, but to be sure to go to a Bible-preaching church. He also warned us that the church we had visited was a cult, which we questioned.

We started reading scripture as we went to bed each night. Then we'd turn off the light and each roll to our side of the bed and pray silently, each of us saying "Amen" out loud as we finished. The following Sunday morning we went to church where Pastor John ministered, and decided to attend their evening service as well. We were astounded to hear people talking about answers to prayer, and singing with joy and enthusiasm both old hymns and some totally new choruses! We decided we'd have to go back there again.

But we also determined that we wanted to pay another visit to the church we had been visiting before our challenge from Pastor John. Could it possibly be a cult? Unsure about which place was preaching the truth, we decided to take seriously our neighbors' church's suggestion to tithe. That morning at their church we presented our tithe with a prayer, "O Father, show us the truth, and we will tithe wherever that leads us." And that morning a member of the congregation invited us to his home for their family home meeting the next evening.

It was an enjoyable evening, and in an attempt to involve us all, the father suggested each of us draw a picture of something meaningful to us personally. Being artistically challenged, I tried to think of something that would be almost impossible to goof up, and decided I could draw an upside down semicircle and put two intersecting lines atop it, creating a cross on top of a hill. It may have been primitive, but at least it fulfilled the requirement. When I held up my drawing, the host's 12-year-old daughter said, “What’s that?” Despite my lack of talent, I knew it should have been evident to anyone that it was a cross on a hill. Her response disquieted both Bob and me.

The next day we told Pastor John what had happened. “There’s your proof!” he exclaimed. “The cross is central to the Christian faith, and in a Christian home even a small child should recognize it. That’s strong proof they’re a cult.” We thankfully recognized God’s swift answer to our prayer.

A couple weeks later, after we had finished our Bible reading and turned off the light, Bob said, “Well, I think I’ve done it; have you?” And I replied, “Yes.” We had both decided separately that day to accept Christ as our Savior!

That was more than half a lifetime ago. Two years after accepting Christ we felt the Lord urging us to go to Bible college. While there my husband received a call from God to enter the ministry. It’s been a real adventure—one that more than answered the “What’s missing?” question for us. And one which we wouldn’t have traded for anyone else’s walk through life.

If you haven’t accepted your need for Christ and asked Him into your life, let me challenge you: For 30 days diligently read the Bible and pray every day, and attend a Bible-preaching church. Then welcome Christ as your Savior and Lord of your life. You’ll find that whether you have a deeply troubled life or a great life with “just something missing,” Jesus truly is the answer.

MAKING CHOICES

Long, long, oh so very long ago, before there were
computers,
or cars,
or fossil digs,
or dinosaurs
There was a beautiful place called heaven.

If you think of the prettiest place you've ever been,
the best day you've ever had,
the nicest people you've ever known,
the most beautiful thing you've ever seen,
and the loveliest dream you've ever dreamed,
Heaven was even better than all of those things put together.

Heaven was, and still is, where God lives. He was there when
He separated day from night,
He flung the stars into space,
He created birds and fish and animals,
And He made the first man and woman.
And time as we know it began.

If you could peek into heaven right now you would see
God the Father sitting on His heavenly throne,
Jesus Christ sitting beside Him, praying for us,
many, many angels singing praises to the Lord,
and joy and peace all around.
But there was a time it wasn't that way.

One time an angel named Satan decided he wanted to replace God.
He changed from being wise and beautiful to being proud.
That was sin.
Heaven would not be the beautiful place it is if sin were there,
so God threw Satan from heaven down to earth.
That's when things here on earth began to change.

Until that time earth had been almost as nice as heaven.
The first man and woman God created lived in a beautiful garden.
God warned them not to eat the fruit of one of its trees.
But when Satan, like a snake, lied and told them
to believe him and not God, they both ate that fruit.
They chose to believe Satan rather than God. What a bad choice they made!

God made them leave that beautiful garden because they had sinned
by ignoring the loving warning He had given them.
They chose to do what *they* wanted instead of what God told them.
They wanted to eat that piece of fruit
more than they wanted to obey what God said.
When they did wrong, or sinned, they found it brought trouble.

Ever since then, that bad angel known as Satan has been trying to
cause people to doubt what God says,
make us turn away from God,
tell lies that sound believable,
and get people to worship him rather than God.
He set up his own way of doing things quite differently from God's ways.

God is wise and kind and patient and loving.
He always does what's right and He never breaks a promise.
He encourages people to be like Him
so life can be nice for everyone.
And guess what?
God wants you and your family to become part of His family.

Satan also wants people to be like himself. But he is
a liar and tries to get others to lie, too.
He tries to convince people not to believe God,
not to care for others, and to put themselves first.
Satan would like you to join his family
to keep you and your family from being part of God's family.

Did you know God sent His only son, Jesus, to die
so we can be forgiven when we sin?
We can accept Jesus into our heart and life
and receive His help to follow God and be part of His family.
It's part of God's plan to help you be all He created you to be.
You can live the kind of life you and God both will like you to live.

Before God even created you or me or anyone, He made a choice.
He decided to give each of us the gift of making choices.
We can choose to be more like Him,
or we can decide to act more like Satan.
Our choices can bring us and others sadness or happiness.
What we choose to do can be *very* important.

The Bible helps people learn to make good choices.
If you show others God's love by loving God, them, and yourself,
and you memorize helpful Bible verses and do what they say–
when you keep doing things like that you'll discover
that following God and the Bible makes it easier to make choices.
And they'll be better choices than you used to make!

Read again about what Satan and God are like. Whose ways do you think would
bring you a better kind of life,
make your mom and dad happier,
give people around you more pleasure,
make the world a nicer place to live,
delight God and the angels, too?

You can make a choice today to do things God's way.
And you can make that choice again every time you wonder what you can do
to show your love for God and others.
How happy that will make the people you help! And you!
And how much joy that will give God, too!
Totally Awesome!

Here's a place to draw or color some ideas you got from that story!

JOY THRIVES IN THE FERTILE SOIL OF A THANKFUL HEART

How To Help It Happen

Through the centuries in locations all over the world Christians have found that, no matter what the circumstances, an individual can always find at least one thing for which to be thankful. Has your home just been destroyed? You're still alive; be thankful for that. Have you just lost all your finances? Man's greatest riches are not money; something for which you can be thankful. Did you just learn that you have a disabling disease? Many means of healing are possible; and your soul can remain healthy as you seek them. Another reason to be thankful.

Examples are endless, and countless people have witnessed themselves or others grasp the importance of seeking—in the midst of any disaster or tragedy—at least one reason for being thankful.

Let's make that Step One: No matter how small the reason to be thankful may seem, find one thing for which to be thankful.

Step Two: Begin to thank God for whatever that reason is, and ask Him to help you recognize other things for which you can thank Him. Then add those reasons. Is anyone else concerned? Thank God for them. Do you have health to help you in your struggle? Thank Him for it. People you can ask for prayer? More to be thankful for! Transportation to go where you may need to go? Something else for which to give thanks. Notice the list keeps growing. That's because our focus is changing from the problem to the Problem Solver.

Step Three: Remember what you know about God. He loves you. He's powerful. He is just. And wise. He's also kind, compassionate, and full of grace and mercy. And that's only a start. Further, God works all things together for good for those who love Him and are called according to His purposes. And what are those purposes? To bring all people into a right relationship with Him for their good and His glory.

Step Four: As your mind and heart center on all these encouraging thoughts, you'll find they provide the fertile soil in which joy takes root and grows.

Step Five: As other serious situations occur, make a conscious effort to repeat steps one through four. In the meantime, as you spend time in the Bible underline or highlight verses that undergird these ideas. Then meditate on them and memorize them. And pass these helpful ideas on to others so they can use them when they, too, confront difficult times.

Scriptural foundation for this article:

Psalm 34:1, " I will bless the LORD at all times; His praise shall continually be in my mouth." (NAS) .

Romans 15:4, " For everything that was written in the past was written to teach us, so that through endurance taught in the Scriptures and the encouragement they provide we might have hope" (NIV).

Philippians 4:4–7, "Rejoice in the Lord always. I will say it again: Rejoice! Let your gentleness be evident to all. The Lord is near. Do not be anxious about anything, but in everything, by prayer and petition, with thanksgiving, present your requests to God. And the peace of God, which transcends all understanding, will guard your hearts and minds in Christ Jesus" (NIV).

Colossians 3:17, "And whatever you do, whether in word or deed, do it all in the name of the Lord Jesus, giving thanks to God the Father through him" (NIV).

Colossians 4:2, "Devote yourselves to prayer, being watchful and thankful" (NIV).

I Thessalonians 5: 16-18, "Be joyful always; pray continually; give thanks in all circumstances, for this is God's will for you in Christ Jesus" (NIV).

Hebrews 13:15, "Through Him then, let us continually offer up a sacrifice of praise to God, that is, the fruit of lips that give thanks to His name: (NAS).

PEACE BE TO THIS HOUSE

Giving or receiving a present is enjoyable for both people involved. Many people have financial difficulties, though, and feel there's no way they can enjoy gift giving. Here's an interesting way Jesus spoke to His disciples about a gift every one of us can give others.

In Luke 10:5–6 (NAS) our Lord told seventy of His followers, "And whatever house you enter, first say, 'Peace be to this house.' And if a man of peace is there your peace will rest upon him; but if not, it will return to you."

What a win-win statement Jesus was instructing His disciples to declare. With one sentence they could bless any place they went with peace if a peaceful person lived there. If not, that peace would return to them. What could they lose?

Does it make you wonder why this isn't practiced by Christians everywhere? Do you remember ever reading or hearing about it being a custom of the church in any nation or any century? Maybe we should start a trend!

Since I have, in a sense, entered your home through this writing, let me say, "Peace be to *this* house." Assuming you are a person of peace, it's nice to know that with this blessing the peace which comes from God will rest upon you. What a gift it enables me to give you – with no shopping, no shipping, no wrapping and no cost involved. My guess is there would be few gifts more appreciated by you or anyone.

An equally great blessing is that Jesus told His disciples *they* could do this. That means that if you're one of His followers He has given *you* the same privilege. Devote some thought and prayer to this privilege. To whom would you like to pass God's peace? With whom would God want you to share it? In the midst of a society in increasing turmoil, it's a great gift to give or receive, isn't it?

EFFORTLESS GRACE

But as it is written in the Scriptures: *"No one has ever seen this, and no one has ever heard about it, no one has ever imagined what God has prepared for those who love him."*
(1 Corinthians 2:9, NCV)

If you could be present at one thing that is happening, has happened, or is yet to take place, what would it be? Would you choose something past tense, present tense, or future tense? What do you think would be the most enticing event to witness?

The covey of questions, designed for website security ID purposes, set my mind adventuring! Wouldn't it be interesting to experience a day in the life of an ancestor centuries or even millennia ago? How difficult was everyday life? Were they part of close-knit communities or was it an every-man-for-himself existence?

Perhaps my choice should be to go far enough into space to be sucked into an impossible-to-anticipate experience in a black hole; or better yet, to go far enough into the future to cross into another galaxy. The multiplicity of ideas seemed limitless.

As I toyed with those fantasies, the idea of being present when God began creating the heavens and the earth seemed like it would be the most amazing of all. To see God start with nothing and simply by speaking create such fantastic change on such a grand scale is more than I can fathom.

Do you know what *sprezzatura* means? It means doing something very well without showing effort. That's how Genesis, the first book in the Bible, infers God created not just the earth but the entire universe! Effortlessly, or with effortless grace. Can we even begin to imagine that?

Yet it is that same effortless grace He extends when He presents us with the offer to begin a personal relationship with Him. When we ask Christ to become our Savior we become one of God's children; adopted into His family. Ah, God's sprezzatura! How easy for us to receive it, but at what tremendous cost Christ bought it for us.

Every person ever born missed seeing the original creation, but what an opportunity Jesus bought for us when He died and rose again so we can become part of the family of God by accepting Christ as our Savior and Lord of our lives.

Here are a couple questions you and your family and/or your friends might enjoy talking about:

If *you* could see something from the past, present, or future, what would you choose and why?

How do you see God's marvelous sprezzatura at work in and/or around you today?

Part 2: PARABLES

INTRODUCTION TO PARABLES

A parable is a story that teaches a lesson about life. Jesus used parables when He taught a very large crowd of His followers as He preached the Sermon on the Mount (found in chapters 5 through 7 in the gospel of Matthew). Yet He also used parables when He was just with His twelve disciples. He obviously considered them an important way to illustrate and help people remember important lessons about life.

Four of the parables in this section are only a few pages long, but one, "Tell Me About God, Grandpa," is *m u c h* longer. Yet they all teach important lessons about life.

Maybe after you've read them you'd like to try writing a parable, too!

TIMMY'S BIG MOVE

"But I don't want to move! I like it here!" Timmy sobbed. "I like my school! I like my friends! I like this house! And I just know there will never be another place like this."

Tears began creeping down his cheeks, and his sobs made his breathing sound like a car trying to start on a cold winter morning.

Lovingly Timmy's dad rested a hand on his shoulder. "Your mom and I are sad about leaving here, too. But my new job means we have to go. And I think you'll like living in the country. Just wait and see."

Timmy continued packing the treasures in his room. His folks had already taken down the posters on his walls, and only a few things remained for him to put into boxes. There was the football he always threw with his buddies after school. And the baseball cards he had traded with the guys in his class. His catcher's mitt, the old teddy he had shaved before he knew not to, and his collection of seashells—he carefully placed them all in the last boxes he had to fill before they would move tomorrow.

He could hear his mom and dad downstairs, talking and laughing as they finished packing in the kitchen. "They can't feel as bad about moving as I do," he thought, "or they wouldn't be able to laugh."

That evening, because all their dishes had been wrapped and stored in moving boxes, Timmy and his parents went out for supper. He had always loved pizza, but tonight he could have been chewing cardboard the way it felt in his mouth. Swallowing it was a major effort.

"You know, we have a real adventure ahead of us," said Tim's dad. "Part of me is excited, but I'll admit part of me is scared."

"You? Scared?" Tim asked. He had never thought his dad would be afraid of anything.

"Sure," his father said, "just a little."

"So am I," sighed Timmy, "but I didn't want to tell you 'cause I thought you might say it was silly."

"It's not silly to be afraid but staying afraid would be wrong," his dad replied.

Timmy took another bite of pizza and noticed that it didn't taste as bad as he had thought at first. "How can I not stay afraid" he asked his father.

"I remember a Bible verse in Proverbs that says, 'In all your ways acknowledge Him,' that means God, ''and He will direct your paths." We try to put God first in our lives; and we prayed a lot about my changing jobs. So we trust God to lead us. And because He loves us very much we know He will help us in everything," Timmy's father explained.

"That goes for me, too, doesn't it, Dad?" Timmy added with relief in his voice.

"It sure does. And just remembering that helps a lot, doesn't it?" his dad responded. "Now, if you'd like that last piece of pizza it's yours, but you better hurry before I grab it."

"Thanks, Dad—for the pizza and for helping me feel better," Timmy grinned as he bit into the last slice. Funny how much better it tasted now that he wasn't so scared, he thought.

That night Timmy and his folks slept on blankets on the floor, because they had taken the beds apart for moving the next day. "Now this begins to feel like an adventure," thought Timmy. "Maybe it won't be so bad after all."

Early the next morning some friends and neighbors came to help them load the truck they had rented for moving their things. In almost no time at all their furniture and boxes filled the back of the truck that had looked so big at first.

"We sure appreciate your help," Timmy's mother told their friends. "We're going to miss every one of you. Be sure to come to see us soon."

"Let's pray before you go," suggested their closest friend, Sam Jones. And everyone bowed their heads and closed their eyes, as they formed a circle and held hands.

"Dear Father," Mr. Jones prayed, "We thank You so much for this family. They are very special to us and to You. Please give them a good trip to their new home. Help them to make new friends who love You, too—and to help many who don't know You come to know Jesus' love. And be with them in all ways until we're together again. Amen."

"Good-bye!" "We love you!" "Don't forget to write!" "Send us pictures of your new place!" everyone seemed to be shouting at once as Timmy and his parents climbed into the truck.

They started down the highway toward their new home, towing their car behind them. Saying good-bye to everyone had been difficult, but now that they were on their way Timmy had to admit to himself that he was getting excited just wondering what the new place would be like.

It was dark when they arrived at their new home, and it seemed so quiet compared to the city they had left that morning. Timmy heard the soft hooting of an owl somewhere nearby, and the barking of a dog off in the distance. He wondered if the other sound he was noticing could be crickets. He had read about them before but never heard one, so he wasn't sure.

Then he looked overhead. "Wow! Look at all the stars!" he whispered with awe. And suddenly he remembered the Bible story about a shepherd boy named David, who must have stood out in the country looking at stars, too. God had been with David—and God had used a star to guide the Wise Men to Jesus when He was born.

A warm, secure feeling crept over Timmy as he continued to gaze at the beautiful night sky. God had put those stars in the sky and God had brought his family to this new place. God loved his family, too, and would be with them whether they lived in a big city or in the country.

Their family's new adventure had just begun this morning, but Timmy was already looking forward to whatever might lie ahead. What might God have in mind for his mom and dad and him to share with others to help them come to understand God's wonderful love for them, too? How excited he was to see whatever new adventures might lie ahead for everyone!

THE BEST RED TENNIES EVER

"They look just like I hoped they would!" Matthew shouted excitedly across the fence to his friend, Jill, who lived next door. "Come and see them!"

Matthew had just gotten a new pair of shoes—red tennies—and boy, was he proud of them!

Jill hurried through the gate between their homes and ran up the walk with Matthew. Once inside the house Matthew slid the shoe box out of the store's sack, threw the lid aside, and crinkled up the tissue surrounding the shoes. Taking off his other shoes he slid his stocking feet into his new, bright red shoes.

"Wonder how fast you'll be able to run in them," Jill pondered. That was all the encouragement Matthew needed. He practically flew out their front door, dashed across their front yard and back, ran a few circles and then headed back to where Jill sat watching him.

"They've got to be the best shoes EVER," Matthew said. "Want to try them on?"

"Sure! I was hoping you'd ask," replied Jill. Off came her own shoes and on went Matthew's bright red tennies. "Oh, no, they're way too big," she wailed as she tried to walk around the room. "I can hardly keep them on my feet. Guess I'll have to leave the running to you."

"Guess so," said Matthew. "But maybe your mom can get you a pair."

Jill lowered her eyes. Matthew thought maybe he even saw a tear. "Not since daddy's out of work," Jill whispered. Mom says we're lucky to have each other and we won't be buying any new clothes until Dad can find a job somewhere."

"Oh, I forgot," Matt replied, lowering his voice in embarrassment.

That night when Matthew went to bed he took his new shoes to bed with him.

"Don't you think you'll be uncomfortable sleeping with your shoes under your arm?" his mother asked.

"Yes, but for one night it's worth it. Tomorrow they'll be dirty from playing outside, so this is my first and last chance. Please, Mom?," he pleaded.

"All right, but just this once. Are you ready to say your prayer now?" she asked as she sat down on the side of his bed.

"Yes, ma'am," he replied, and began to pray. "Dear God, thank you for my new shoes. And for mama and daddy who bought them for me. And for my friend Jill. And, God, please help Jill's daddy get a new job so they can have new clothes, too. Amen"

Matthew's mother leaned over and kissed him good night.

"Mama, can God help Jill's dad get a different job?" Matthew questioned.

"If we pray and he tries, I'm sure the Lord will help him," she answered softly.

"Well, why did God let him not have a job?"

"It says in the Bible that all things work together for good. And that means that whatever happens to people who love God, God can make something good come from it for them. If they trust God He will use it to strengthen their faith. Sometimes it happens quickly, but other times it seems to take much longer than we hoped it would."

"Do you remember when you broke your arm last summer?" she asked.

"Do I ever! Nothing ever hurt me as much as that did!" Matthew clenched his teeth as he recalled how much it hurt.

His mom smiled as she reminded him of the unanticipated result. "But that's when we met Dr. Albert in the emergency room. And as he worked on your arm we all talked and we invited him to come to church and . . . "

" . . . and he accepted Jesus!" Matthew finished her sentence excitedly.

"I get it!" he added. "When we think something's real bad, if we pray and love God and trust Him, He somehow makes something good out of it. Sort of like recycling!" The words tumbled over one another almost as fast as his feet had flown when he raced around in his new tennies earlier.

"I couldn't have said it any better myself," his mother replied as she gave him a big hug.

"One more thing, Mom."

"What's that, my little man?"

"I know God can do a lot. But I remember Jesus said we're to love our neighbor as much as we love ourselves. Let's see if Jill would like a pair of shoes like mine—and we'll get them for her, okay? I've saved some money from my allowance, and I think it would be more fun doing that than anything else I can think of."

"I'm very proud of you," his mother smiled, as she gave him another hug and kiss. "Good night, dear. God bless you."

"'Nite, Mom. God bless you, too," he mumbled as he snuggled into his covers and quickly fell asleep.

When he woke the next morning Matthew's first thought was what a wonderful day this was going to be because of the idea God had given him to get Jill some tennies like his. That would make his parents proud and happy. And Jill's happiness with the new red tennies and Matthew's kindness would make both her parents happy also.

What a wonderful way for people to experience God's love. It's why Jesus told people they should treat one another the way they would like to be treated.

Matthew and his parents did a wonderful job of showing God's love.

How do you think you're doing? How would other people say you're doing?

HERE, KITTY, KITTY

"Here, Kitty, Kitty, Kitty," Andrew called. In almost no time at all his beloved tabby cat Peekaboo appeared and began her gentle figure-eight weaving around his ankles, leaning first to one side and then the other.

Andrew sat down on the back porch steps and began talking to his furry feline friend. She was like a best friend 'cause he could tell her anything and know she would listen and love him no matter what. And he didn't need to worry about her telling anyone anything he said.

Today he was telling her about a Bible study he had stayed after school to attend. He liked the songs they sang since he loved music. And the games they played were new but fun. But when the teacher began talking about having to always do what was right 'cause if you didn't "God is gonna get you" it was scary! Most of the time Andrew tried to obey what his parents told him to do, and he tried to be nice, but he knew he sure wasn't perfect.

"Peekaboo, I'm scared," he confessed as she cocked her head to one side and listened attentively, appearing to be as concerned as Andrew was. He affectionately petted the "M" on her forehead, heaved a big sigh, and said, "Thanks for being such a good listener. If you could talk I'd love to hear what you think." Her soft purring as she continued rubbing against his ankles helped him feel a little calmer.

As Andrew went inside, he began sharing with his parents what was bothering him. Guess what his mom and dad did? They both said, "We need to pray about this!" Papa prayed first. "Father God, we know You love us; after all, You created us. And You don't want Andrew or anyone to be scared of You. so we ask You to help us find some scriptures to help assure Andrew of Your wonderful love and care for all of us."

And Andrew's mother added thanks to Papa's request as she prayed, "Lord, we know the best gift You have given the three of us is being a family that shares our love of You, each other, and the Bible. And we delight in sharing those blessings with everyone we can as You guide us. Thank You that the Bible promises us You'll answer our prayers."

That night after supper Andrew told his folks, "God's already helped me feel less scared. I want to ask Him to help the kids who looked as scared as I felt but maybe don't have parents they can talk to. They need help to have the peace I'm feeling now." And he prayed about it right away.

With a pad of sticky notes Andrew and his mom and dad made sticky notes with Bible verses on them that he could hand to the students he knew had been at the study where the scary, not-true-to-scripture thought was spoken. In case you're ever in a place where others hear scary, rather than loving, things said about God, maybe you'd like to share these verses with them so God's love will help them, too, to erase those wrong thoughts:

"For God loved so loved the world, that he gave his only Son, that whoever believes in him should not perish but have eternal life. For God did not send His Son into the world to condemn the world, but in order that the world might be

saved through Him. Whoever believes in Him is not condemned. . . . " (John 3:16-18a ESV).

"For I know the plans I have for you, declares the LORD, plans for welfare and not for calamity, to give you a future and a hope" (Jeremiah 29:11 NAS).

"Cast all your anxiety on him because he cares for you" (1 Peter 5:7 NIV).

"We love because He first loved us" (1 John 4:19 NIV).

If something like this happens to you, share it with a family member or friend who loves you, God and His Word. Instead of being hurt by the experience, you can grow in the Lord. PTL!

FROM THE BOOK, TELL ME ABOUT GOD, GRANDPA

Chapter One

"I got one! I got one!" Joshua shouted with delight as he felt his fishing pole jerk and saw it bend toward the water.

Joshua's grandfather grabbed the fishing net and held it under Josh's line as he lifted the wiggling fish from its cold, wet home. "Looks like we can have some nice fresh fish for supper tonight," Grandpa said. "Shall we ask Grandma to fix it or shall I make a campfire and we can cook it out of doors?"

"O-o-o-h, let's cook outside! Then we can make s'mores for dessert. Oh, boy, I can hardly wait!"

Joshua and his grandfather picked up their fishing poles and bait and began the short walk to Grandma and Grandpa's place. Josh whistled a happy tune as they walked the block from the small lake to the camper home where Grandpa and Grandma spent their summers. Getting to spend his first week ever here without his mom and dad sure made him feel special.

As soon as they got to the camper, Joshua showed his catch to Grandma, and then Grandpa cleaned it and began making the campfire. It seemed like no time at all until Grandpa called, "Dinner's ready!" and Grandma had Joshua help her carry baked potatoes and corn-on-the-cob and a salad to the picnic table.

After they were all seated Grandpa and Grandma bowed their heads and Grandpa said a prayer to thank God for providing a great meal for them. How wonderful everything tasted! All of them agreed that no fish ever tasted as good as freshly caught fish cooked over a campfire. When Joshua got to make his own s'more with no help at all for the first time, he decided that being almost eight years old really made him feel like he was growing up.

Joshua helped his grandma and grandpa carry the dirty dishes into the camper. As Grandma washed and Joshua dried the dishes, Grandpa made sure the fire was completely out and then set up stakes so they could play a game of horseshoes. Josh loved playing this game. Even though he knew he couldn't pitch a horseshoe as far as Grandpa could, last year he had been able to throw almost as far as Grandma. He was eager to see if maybe, just maybe, he could beat her at least once this year. And if he was really lucky he might even come close to tying with Grandpa.

Do you think our yard's big enough to play horseshoes?" he asked his grandparents.

"Oh, I'm sure it is," said his grandmother. "Maybe that would be a good gift to ask for on your next birthday."

"That's just what I was thinking. I think all the guys that live near me would like pitchin' horseshoes. It'd be more fun than TV or computer games 'cause we'd be outside and get to use our muscles."

Grandpa and Grandma both laughed and Grandma said, "Would you believe we didn't even have TVs or computers when we were your age?"

"While you're here this week maybe you'd like to do some of the things with us that we used to do to have fun when we were kids. How does that sound?" Grandpa asked.

"Cool," Joshua said. "That sounds real cool. Sort of. I can't imagine what you could do that was fun before computers or televisions were made. Sounds to me like we might get bored quick."

"Well, we'll try not to let that happen," Grandpa chuckled.

After a few games of horseshoes Grandma suggested they sit and watch the sun as it was setting for the night. How beautiful the sky looked with all the different shades of gold and red stretching as far right and left as they could see, and glowing softly as the sun disappeared below the horizon.

As it got darker and darker they noticed first one star and then another begin to sparkle above them. How black the night sky looked at first. But as they watched more and more stars lit up the night sky. Joshua could hardly believe how many stars there were overhead! Grandma pointed out to him the stars that formed the Big Dipper.

"It's like a follow-the-dots picture in the sky!" Joshua exclaimed excitedly.

"Do you see the stars over there to the north that look like a large, spread-out W?" Grandpa asked as he sketched the starry outline above them with his forefinger. That's a constellation known as Cassiopeia, or The Queen. There's a story in mythology that says she was such a beautiful goddess she got thrown into the sky, but because she became so proud she was turned upside down part of the year to help rid her of her pride."

"What did you call that?"

"I'm not sure which thing you're asking about, but a group of stars that forms a picture is called a constellation. And that constellation, known as The Queen, has the name Cassiopeia. And mythology is a collection of myths or make-believe stories from long, long ago. Any more questions?"

"Uh-huh. You can tell you taught, Grandpa. That reminded me of something Mrs. Underwood would have said in science class. But I have a question: Why don't I see these at home? We go out in our backyard for cookouts, too, but I've never noticed so many stars at one time before."

"You live in a city, and the lights of all the big buildings and electronic displays and traffic, make so much light that the light from the stars can't be seen. Out here there isn't much in the way of man-made light, so the stars can be seen in all their glory."

"Wow! Neat!" Rubbing his neck as he adjusted his gaze from the spectacular stars to their little campsite, Joshua saw the off and on blinking of fireflies. "It's almost like they're trying to light up the yard the way the stars light up the sky," he said, smiling at the thought.

"If you'd like to, the night before you leave for home you can catch some of those lightning bugs to take with you," Grandma said. "How does that sound?"

Trying to stifle a yawn, Joshua nodded his head. "Sounds great," he said, and smiled sleepily.

Noticing his drowsiness, Grandpa stood up. "Time for a bath and bedtime before your grandma and I fall asleep out here and you have to carry us both to bed." He laughed a hearty laugh and Joshua giggled as he pictured that happening. Then Grandpa took Joshua's hand in his, put his other arm around Grandma, and they all walked toward the camper.

Chapter Two

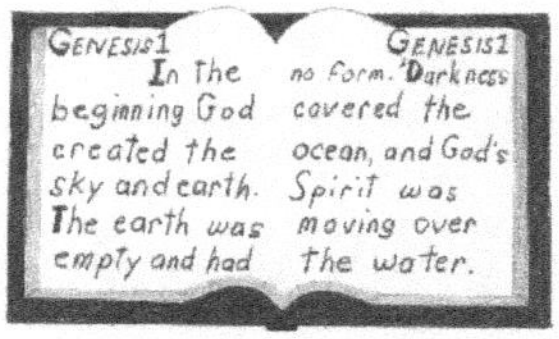

The next morning Joshua lay in bed trying to decide if Grandma and Grandpa were awake yet. Hearing no sounds coming from the kitchen, he tiptoed in that direction.

As he looked into the front room he saw Grandpa sitting in his favorite chair with a book open in his lap. "Whatcha readin', Grandpa?" he asked.

"My favorite book, the Bible," Grandpa answered with a smile on his face that told Joshua his grandpa was really enjoying it.

"What's it about?" Joshua questioned.

"It's about God. And every time I read it I learn more about Him. It's full of stories, but they aren't make-believe stories like lots of books have. They're stories about things that really happened. Like how the earth was made. Or about real people—like Noah, who built a huge boat to keep animals safe in during a flood. Or Daniel, who was thrown into a large hole in the ground that had lions in it, but God kept them from hurting him. And Jesus, God's Son, who came to teach people about God and show us how much He loves us.

"That sounds awesome, Grandpa. Will you read me some of those stories. And can you tell me about God, Grandpa?

"Josh, there's nothing I'd enjoy more than telling you about God. I have an idea! Remember last night how Grandma and I said we'd do something different every day while you're here that we used to do for fun with our friends when we were young?"

"Yeah, but how does that tell me about God?"

"It doesn't. But I thought that maybe, just like we decided to do that, you might like to hear about God a little each day, too.

"Sounds good to me. But could I have some cereal, please?" Joshua asked.

"Of course! Think I'll have some with you." Grandpa said as he got a couple of boxes of cereal for Joshua to choose from. "And how about some orange juice?"

"Okay!" Joshua said as he dropped into a table-side chair. "I know you're not looking at your Bible, but could you tell me one of those Bible stories while we're eating breakfast?"

"Absolutely!" Grandpa responded enthusiastically. "While I was going to sleep last night I was thinking about how much the three of us enjoyed looking at the stars. Well, God made those stars."

"No kidding!" Joshua stopped his spoon half-way to his mouth. "How did He do that?"

"He only needed to speak and they were created. He also made the earth we live on and everything on it. In fact, there's nothing that exists, nothing you can see or hear, that wasn't made by Him. And that's why we call Him our Creator."

"He even made fireflies?"

"Yep!"

"And cats and dogs?"

"Yes, cats and dogs, too."

"And bugs and bears and butterflies, and. . . "

"Absolutely! Anything you can think of was made by God. He even made the food we eat and the air we breathe."

"Awesome!" Joshua had resumed eating, though he obviously was impressed. "Did He make this cereal we're eating?"

"Well, not exactly. But God made the grain and the sugar beets and other ingredients that people used to make it. And if He hadn't done that we couldn't be eating it."

"Did He make you and Grandma and me and all the other people, too?"

"That's sort of like what I told you about the cereal. While it takes a man and a woman to make a baby, God is the One who made the first man and woman so they could have children. And from those first two people, Adam and Eve, all of us have eventually been born."

"Sounds like I'm missing out on quite a discussion," Grandma said as she walked into the kitchen and started making coffee.

"Grandpa was telling me about things God created," Joshua spoke up excitedly. "Did you know that He made EVERYTHING?"

"I sure did!" Grandma replied. "Isn't our heavenly Father wonderful?"

"Our heavenly Father? Who is that?" Joshua asked. "I thought Grandpa was telling me about God."

Grandma leaned over and kissed Joshua on the top of his head. "'Heavenly Father' is just one of the names people use when they talk about God. His Son Jesus called Him that and let us know we can, too, because God loves us just like all good fathers love their children."

"Neat! So in a way I have two fathers!"

"Yes, the one you've always known, who your mommy is married to, and also your Father in heaven, who is God. Do you remember the picture we have of you when you were real little, and you were standing in a pair of your daddy's shoes? You wanted so much to be like him," Grandma said, smiling as she pictured one of her favorite snapshots. "Your dad was so proud you tried to imitate him. And now you watch your dad and do a lot of things he does.

"You know, God would like His children to see what He's like and then be like Him, too. It makes Him proud and happy if you imitate Him, just like it makes your dad feel when you try to do what he does"

Joshua squinted as he tried to figure it out. "But how can I be like God when I can't see Him?"

"Good question, Joshua! The answer is that we can see what God is like by reading the Bible!" Grandpa chimed in.

"Do they have pictures of Him in there?"

"They don't have pictures like you put in a frame, but they have what you could call word pictures. They don't show us what God looks like, but they tell us what He's like. They tell us He's good, and wise, and patient, and just, or fair, and forgiving. We learn that God never lies or breaks a promise. He also knows what's in our hearts," Grandma added. "But there's so much more that word pictures tell us about God that I think maybe we should wait until tomorrow for that. We need to get dressed and do one of those old-time things before it gets too hot.

"All right!" Joshua shouted, jumping up from the table. "I'll be the first one ready to go!"

"Honey," Grandpa lowered his voice as he spoke, "maybe Joshua's parents won't be pleased when they learn that we're sharing with him about Jesus."

"I've thought about that and you're right," she agreed. "But look how eager Josh is to learn about God and the Bible. Let's pray his parents will be, too."

"Of course, I should have thought of that," Grandpa said as he reached for her hand and began to pray. "Father, we know You love Joshua even more than we do. And we're thankful that You also love his parents. We're so pleased You're giving us the joy of telling Josh about You. Work in his mom's and dad's hearts to join him in the desire to know more about You and Your wonderful plan for their lives. Thank You for this day with Josh. Help us to recognize the opportunities you give us to share Your love with him and others. Amen."

Chapter Three

It was mid-morning when Grandpa, Grandma and Joshua arrived at the small building where canoes could be rented. "Just a two-hour rental, please," Grandpa told the young person in charge.

"Thank you, sir," she answered politely. She took his money and pointed to where several canoes lay waiting. Grandpa and Grandma looked at a few of the canoes and chose a cheerful orange one. The young lady who rented the canoe to them reminded them to be sure to put on their life jackets before they left.

"Should we go if it's dangerous?" Joshua asked.

"Good thinking," Grandpa said, "but where we'll be going there's not much to worry about. We won't be hitting rough water or making our way around big tree roots or rocks. But it'll still give you an idea of what canoeing's like. That's something we used to do a lot when we were teenagers."

"Very cool," Joshua said as they each put on a life jacket. He and Grandma got in the canoe, and Grandpa shoved it away from the shore and jumped in.

Joshua was perched on the small seat in the front of the canoe, Grandma sat on the middle seat, and Grandpa paddled from the back. After a few minutes Grandma turned around and said to Grandpa, "How about handing me one of those paddles?"

Grandpa leaned forward carefully and held out a paddle to Grandma. "Which side do you want to paddle on?" he asked.

"The left, if that's okay with you," she replied over her shoulder.

"Okay, let's show our grandson how to get a little more speed out of one of these," Grandpa said as Grandma began rowing in rhythm with him."

To Joshua's surprise the canoe really did pick up speed with two people paddling. "Can I try it? Can I?" he pleaded with them.

"Let us keep the rhythm going for a while so you get the feel of what you need to do when you take my place," Grandma suggested.

After what seemed to Josh like forever, Grandpa asked, "Think you've got the picture?"

"I sure do! Just give me your paddle, Grandma!"

Joshua stood up, swang around quickly, and reached back for the paddle. He froze in mid-air when he felt the canoe begin to tilt from side to side. "What did I do wrong?" he asked with alarm, afraid to move a muscle.

"It's okay, don't worry. It just shows you how little it takes to tip a canoe. But as long as you're careful and don't move too quickly we'll be fine," Grandpa assured him.

Joshua grasped the paddle Grandma held out for him, eased down onto his seat, and began his turn helping Grandpa to paddle the canoe. At first his strokes seemed to just skim the top of the water. "It's not as easy as it looks," he said. "How do you do this?"

"Try to hold the paddle a little more up and down instead of so flat," called Grandpa. "I'll slow down a little and we'll see if that helps." And it did!

Joshua was delighted to feel himself actually paddling the canoe with his Grandpa. He felt so excited he would have liked to jump up and down. But he remembered how the canoe had tipped back and forth when all he had done was stand to reach back for the paddle. So he decided he'd wait until he was on dry ground to do the jumping up and down.

How quiet things were as the canoe slipped almost silently through the water. Not many other people seemed to be taking advantage of the beautiful day to spend time on the lake. It was nice to have this part of it almost to themselves.

It wasn't long before Joshua found himself wearing out. "My arms are starting to get tired," he said with disappointment in his voice.

"You've been doing real well. But I wondered how long you could keep it up. Would you like me to take over again for a while?" Grandma offered.

"Can I have a turn again before we have to take the canoe back?

"Sure," Grandma told him. "Just hand the paddle back to me and I'll take your place for a little bit."

This time the trade went more smoothly and she and Grandpa resumed their rhythmical paddling.

"Now that you're not busy paddling you can relax and look around," Grandpa suggested to Joshua. "Had you noticed that it's cooler when we go under the shade of a tree? And did you see how many different creatures enjoy being along the edges of the lake?"

"Guess I wasn't paying attention to anything but trying to learn to paddle," Joshua said. He bit into an apple he had brought along and began to look around.

"Look at that bird with long legs, standing on only one foot over there. He looks so funny!" Joshua laughed out loud and was surprised to see the bird fly away at the sound of his laughter. "Oops, I didn't mean to scare him. Sorry, bird."

"That was a whooping crane," Grandpa informed him, and then took a glance at his watch. "Looks like we need to be turning around before long so we can get this canoe back before our time's up. Let's make a turn to the left just after we pass that tree. Okay, dear?"

"Okay, honey."

This time Joshua noticed how it did feel cooler as they passed into the shade of the huge tree that bordered the lake and then warmed again as soon as its shadow no longer protected them. "Cool," he whispered, as though he thought speaking might shatter the pleasure of it all.

"Would you like to just float without rowing for a while, and enjoy the quiet for a bit?" Grandpa offered after they had made the turn.

"I'd love it," Grandma answered.

"So would I," chorused Joshua.

Grandpa and Grandma drew their paddles into the canoe and it drifted to almost a standstill. Not even one other canoe was in sight. Joshua closed his eyes and listened to the sounds around them. Somewhere off in the distance he heard the faint sound of a car horn. And a dog barking. And then he heard nothing but the rustle of a light breeze in the leaves of a tree on the shoreline. A nearby splash surprised him, but Grandpa said it probably was just the sound of a fish dropping back into the water after a big jump. Or it might have been a frog.

Joshua opened his eyes and looked around. First he saw another of those birds standing on one leg. What did Grandpa say they were? Oh, yeah, whooping cranes. Then he spotted three chipmunks that looked like they were playing tag. He would have laughed out loud at the chipmunks, but he remembered how his laugh had scared the whooping crane away earlier, so he put his hand over his mouth just in time. What else might he see?

He looked overhead and spied two smaller birds gliding on the wind's currents. As he lowered his gaze he noticed the lovely blue of some flowers that grew close to the ground, and a cluster of bulrushes hugging the bank of the lake. Two ducks were lazily floating in the shadow of the bulrushes. Looking even more closely, he noticed there were several smaller ducks almost hidden in the shadows right behind them, following their parents like mirror images. "How cool!" he thought.

"Are you okay, Josh?" Grandpa asked.

"Uh-huh. I was just trying to take a picture with my mind so I can remember this forever," Joshua said quietly. "I wish I could paint a picture that would look like this. I know you told me this morning that God created everything. He sure did a good job, didn't He?"

"Absolutely!" Grandma and Grandpa said at the same time.

Grandpa began paddling again. "If you want to do any more paddling with me this is probably a good time," Grandpa suggested.

This time the transfer of the paddle between Grandma and Joshua went so smoothly you would have thought the three of them had canoed together for a long time. Joshua was surprised and pleased that he was able to help with the paddling all the way to where they needed to drop off the canoe. As Grandpa steered it into the bank of the lake, he asked Josh, "Do you think you could hop out and pull the canoe a little farther forward onto the land while I push us ahead with my paddle?"

"Sure, Grandpa," Joshua said confidently as he gingerly made his way to the front of the canoe. He eased himself onto the wet, muddy ground, and picked up the rope, tugging as hard as he could while Grandpa pushed with the paddle. Then Joshua tied the best knot he knew how around the pole just ahead of them.

"Great job, my boy," Grandpa said proudly as he got out of the canoe and then turned to help Grandma climb out. "Just let me tie that knot a little more securely and we'll be ready to go. Did you enjoy yourself?"

"Did I ever! It was so cool that if we didn't even do any more old-fashioned things it would be okay. But I hope we will, because I can hardly wait to see what other neat stuff you and Grandma did in the good old days."

"Three more days to do at least three more old-fashioned things. Think we can come up with that many old-timey ideas, Grandma?"

Grandma looked at Grandpa and then at Joshua, and with a twinkle in her eyes, but without saying a word, she smiled a great big smile at both of them.

"Now I can hardly wait for tomorrow!" Joshua said excitedly as he ran toward the car.

Chapter Four

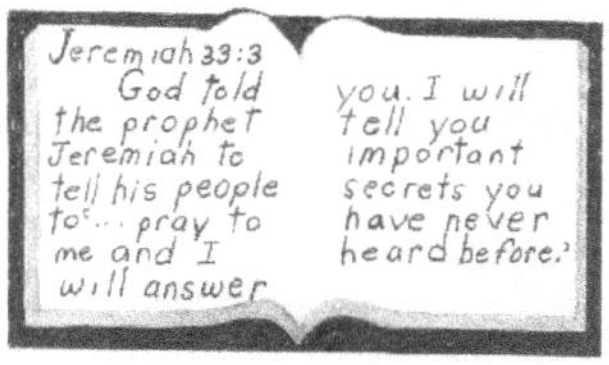

Jeremiah 33:3
God told the prophet Jeremiah to tell his people to'... pray to me and I will answer
you. I will tell you important secrets you have never heard before.'

Joshua woke the next morning to the soft pitter-patter of rain. "Oh, no," he thought, "there's no way we can have fun today with it raining." He threw back his covers, slid out of bed, and hurried toward where he knew he would find Grandpa reading his Bible. To his surprise Grandma was also there with a Bible in her lap. "I didn't know you both liked to read the Bible," he said.

"It's my favorite book, too," Grandma said.

"And she probably could tell you as much about God as I can," Grandpa added. "It looks like we'll be staying inside for a while this morning. Maybe after we have breakfast we could both help you learn more about God."

"And speaking of breakfast, how would a vegetable omelet and some toast and tomato juice sound to you this morning?" Grandma asked.

Both Grandpa and Joshua voted in favor of that menu, and as Grandma began to break eggs into a dish Grandpa began dicing up some red and green peppers and mushrooms and onions. Joshua filled three glasses with tomato juice. "Can I make the toast, too?" he asked.

"Sure!" Grandma answered as she began beating just a little bit of water into the eggs. "Are the veggies ready?" she asked Grandpa.

"All ready. Shall I cook this morning and you do dishes, or do you want to cook and I'll do dishes?"

"Why don't we let you cook, and then you and Joshua can set up a board game while I do dishes."

"Okay," Grandpa agreed as he grabbed a big skillet, sprayed it, set it on the largest burner, and then poured the egg mixture in after the skillet was warm enough. After the eggs had cooked a bit Grandpa poured the vegetables onto one half of them, slid a broad spatula underneath the other half and folded those eggs over on top of the vegetables.

Joshua's eyes lit up with anticipation. "Wow!' he sighed.

A couple minutes later Grandpa made a quick move forward with the skillet, then up and back, and the omelet flipped over in the air all by itself. As it was falling, Grandpa reached under the omelet with the skillet just in time to catch it and return it to the burner. "That was awesome, Grandpa!" Josh said as Grandpa smiled with obvious delight at his admirer.

"Showoff!" Grandma teased. "He knows I can't do that, and it's another reason I had him cook this morning. I thought you'd enjoy that, Joshua."

"It was awesome! Oh, should I put the bread in the toaster now?"

"Great idea! And while Grandpa cuts the omelet into three pieces I'll get some shredded cheese to sprinkle on it, and then breakfast will be ready."

"Looks like we make a pretty good team in the kitchen, just like we did in the canoe," Grandpa commented as they all sat down to eat. "Now let's thank the Lord for this great-looking food."

The three of them closed their eyes and bowed their heads as Grandpa prayed. "We give you thanks, Father, for blessing us with food that helps us to be healthy and happy, and tastes delicious, and for the joy we had working together to prepare it. You are so kind and good, and we love you for blessing us so much. In Jesus' name. Amen."

"Grandpa, why do we pray before we eat?" Joshua questioned as he buttered his toast.

Let me answer your question by asking you a question," Grandpa replied. "If I did nice things for you, would you thank me?"

"Sure!"

"Remember that yesterday we talked about God making everything?"

"Uh-huh."

"Well, that includes the things that go into all that we eat—just like we talked about when you were eating your cereal yesterday, remember?"

"Uh-huh."

"So why not thank our Father in heaven for being nice to us by giving us such delicious things to eat?"

"Oh, I see. But does He really listen to us when we do that?"

"He certainly does. He listens whenever we talk to Him. Your Grandma and I talk to Him every day. Some days we even talk to Him lots of different times."

"But what is there to talk about?" Joshua inquired as he pierced a big bite of omelet with his fork.

"Just about anything you can think of. After we read our Bibles we might spend half an hour talking to God. We might thank Him for something we especially appreciated reading. We could thank Him for the beautiful day and good health. And then we might pray for people we know who are sick; and for missionaries. They're people who often go to other countries to tell people about God and Jesus. And we always pray for our kids and grandkids."

"That's nice," Joshua interjected with a smile.

Grandpa smiled back at him, took a swallow of his juice, and continued. "Sometimes we ask God to forgive our country for some things it has done that weren't things that would please Him. And we might thank Him for our freedom, and ask Him to bless our men and women in the military, and our President and other people who govern our country. Oh, my, I could tell you even more that we pray about, but I think you get the idea."

"Yeah, I think so. But how do you know He even listens to what you and Grandma say?"

"Grandma, we don't mean to be leaving you out of this. Why don't you answer that question for Joshua?" Grandpa replied as he began eating again.

"Joshua, two things prove to us God listens. One is that the Bible tells us He does. A lot of verses tell us that, but probably my favorite is Jeremiah 33:3. God told Jeremiah to tell His people to '. . . pray to Me, and I will answer you. I will tell you important secrets you have never heard before.'"

"The other way that we know," Grandma added, "is that we have seen God answer prayers many times.

"That's awesome," Joshua said. "But I have a friend, Mike, whose mother got cancer last year and he said he prayed for her but she died. So he's mad at God. And it sort of makes me wonder: If God answers your prayers why didn't He answer Mike's?"

"That's a real good question, Joshua. Even a lot of grownups wonder about things like that. Some of them have gotten angry with God, too, and given up learning about Him because they couldn't figure it out," Grandma said. "And if people have never really understood what an awesome God He is in so many ways, it's no wonder they give up."

"What we believe is that most people have never learned about what a great character God has," Grandpa chimed in.

"Huh? What does that mean?" asked Joshua, who had barely noticed that he and his grandparents had all finished eating breakfast by this time.

Grandma nodded to Grandpa that she'd be glad to let him talk as she began removing the dishes that now sat empty in front of them. "Your character is who you are," he explained. "It has a lot to do with your mind, your feelings and your actions. If you were to describe someone you know, without talking about their looks, you would be telling us about their character. Are they angry a lot, or are they patient? Do they think about others first, or are they selfish? If they are strong, do they use their strength to help others or to hurt them? Do their actions show them to be smart or not?"

"How did you learn all those kinds of things about God?" Joshua asked as he gazed out the sliding glass door at the neighbor's cat playing with a June bug.

"That's one reason we enjoy reading the Bible so much," Grandma replied joyfully, as she began washing dishes. "God wants us to know Him and so He has had many different people write many different things to help us learn about Him.

"I still don't understand how knowing that helps," Joshua confessed as the cat he was watching abandoned the bug and began climbing a tree.

"Do you think you know me pretty well?" asked Grandpa?

"Sure. That's a silly question."

"If someone told you that I had stolen their lawn mower would you believe them?"

"Of course not!"

"If someone said I had told them a lie, what would you think?"

"They made a mistake, 'cause you don't tell lies."

"What if they said they saw me hit Grandma, what about that?"

"You would never hit Grandma! You love her too much!" Joshua replied defensively.

"That's exactly right," Grandpa said with a broad smile. "But how can you be so sure about those things?"

"Because I know you!" Joshua said emphatically.

"And that's exactly what we're saying. You know my character. And from reading the Bible and talking with God in prayer and watching Him answer prayer, we know His character. So we've learned that we can trust Him. If we don't get the answer we hoped and prayed for it's because He has something better in mind."

"But I think if I tried to tell Mike that he'd probably be mad at me and never want me to talk to him again," Josh responded as he watched the cat leap from the tree to the neighbor's patio and skitter inside when their screen door opened.

"It's possible that Mike would be angry," Grandpa continued, "but if you feel very strongly that Mike needs your help and God's help, then you can begin asking God to give you the right time and the right way to talk to Mike. And as you keep showing Mike that you care about him God will give you an opportunity."

"Well, guys, I'm through doing dishes, Grandma said. "If you're ready to move on to other things, I'll get out some old games, since it's still raining. Hopefully it will stop raining so we won't have to forget about the walk we want to take around the campground tonight."

"Only one more thing first, Honey," Grandpa said. "Let's pray for Joshua's friend before we start playing games, okay?"

"Of course. I'm glad you thought of that," she answered, and bowed her head.

"Father God," Grandpa began, "we are so glad you've given Joshua a caring heart for his friend Mike's problem. We know you want Mike to come to know you and experience the help he needs to get over the hurt of his mother's death. Please help him see that Joshua cares about his hurting. And give Joshua the opportunity to talk to him about you and your love for him and for His mother. In Jesus' Name. Amen."

"Thank you, Grandpa. I'm so glad to be here. I'm having such a good time. And I'm glad you can tell me things about God."

"And now to the games," Grandma said as she entered the kitchen and placed a stack of boxes on the table."

Chapter Five

"Checkers. Dominoes. Bingo. Old Maid." Joshua counted on his fingers as he named the games they had played. "Oh, and Chinese Checkers, too. That makes at least five games. Did I miss any?"

"Well, I don't remember for sure," said Grandpa, "but I enjoyed the teasing and the laughing even more than the games. I see it's stopped raining and I'd love to go out and stretch my legs. Anyone want to go with me?"

"I do!" Joshua exclaimed, heading for the door.

The rest of the day passed as quickly as the morning had. "This has been another great day," Josh observed after they finished their evening meal. "Didn't you say something about taking a walk tonight? Why is that old fashioned? My mom and dad take lots of power walks."

"Aha! That's it." Grandpa told him. "There are power walks and there are friendship walks. You know what a power walk is about; it's to help you stay or get healthy. But a friendship walk—well, let's just take ours and you can see for yourself. They're both good for you, but boy are they different!" Grandpa told him. "Let me grab our flashlight before we go because it might be dark by the time we head back home."

As they left home Grandpa and Grandma walked right down the middle of their street. "Don't do that. You're going to get run over!" Joshua begged them as he kept to the grassy areas. To his surprise they both laughed at him.

"Take a look around," Grandpa told him. "How many cars do you see moving here in the campground?" Joshua took a quick glance around them and realized he only saw one car being driven, and that was a couple streets away.

Grandma pointed to a sign they were passing: "20 mph" was written on it in large numbers.

"Oh," Joshua observed. "Not many people driving and you can't drive more than 20 miles an hour. No wonder you weren't worried. And no wonder there aren't sidewalks here, either. People can walk in the streets safely."

"We do keep our ears open, because once in a while there will be someone who isn't used to that speed limit and doesn't notice they're going too fast. But everyone walks leisurely on the road. And notice what else they do," Grandma said as she waved to a lady sitting on her front porch and called out to her, "How did that pie recipe work for you, Edith?"

"Best chocolate pie I ever made," the lady called back to her. "Thanks so much! The ladies I play bridge with loved it."

A little farther down the road Grandpa began a conversation with a man mowing his lawn. The man had stopped his mower when he saw them approaching, and Grandpa walked a little faster, moving ahead to shake hands with him. Grandpa greeted him with a question, "Hey, Herb, I see you got your mower fixed. What did you find was wrong with it?"

"Oh, the spark plug and the air filter needed cleaned. It's running fine now."

"Glad to hear it. I'd like you to meet our grandson, Joshua. He's spending the week with us, and we're enjoying every minute of it."

"Joshua, this is Mr. McCoy. The McCoys are from Ohio."

"I'm glad to meet you, young man," Mr. McCoy said as he extended his hand to shake Joshua's.

"Thank you, sir. I'm glad to meet you, too. I don't know just where Ohio is, but I've heard of the Ohio State Buckeyes. Did you ever see them play?"

"Yep, a couple of times. Not a bad team. My wife likes to go to their games because she thinks they've got a great band."

"So do I" Grandma offered. "And where is Jane this evening?"

"Oh, she's out walking, too. She grabbed her harmonica and said something about heading for the Johnsons' place. I'll probably go over there when I finish working on our yard," Mr. McCoy offered.

"That's good to hear! We'll walk over that way now. Hope to see you later."

When they got to the next corner they turned left, saw two ladies walking the opposite direction, each with a dog on a leash, and stopped to pet the dogs and chat with the ladies a couple minutes. Then an older couple riding a bicycle built for two rode by and said "Hi" to them.

At the following corner Grandma and Grandpa stopped to talk with a little old lady trimming her plants as her husband sat in a wheelchair watching. "Your roses are looking so lovely, Frances," Grandma encouraged her as they passed.

"Thank you so much, dear. It's a lovely evening to be outside working."

"And walking," Grandma added with a warm smile. "Hi, Frank! It's nice to see you're able to be outside tonight, too," she added, with a wave to Frances' husband as they walked on by.

"Do you guys know everyone?" Joshua asked, emphasizing the last word of his question.

"No, not all the folks, but quite a few of them. That's why we call our walks friendship walks," Grandpa explained. "But you could call them old-fashioned walks, because as we were growing up families often took walks in the evening. There wasn't air conditioning then, and getting outside was a good way to enjoy the slowly cooling outdoor air and visit with your neighbors at the same time."

By this time they had come to the last camper on the street, where several people were sitting out front. Two guys were tuning up guitars and a lady was tuning a fiddle. Joshua figured the lady with a harmonica in her hand must be Mr. McCoy's wife, Jane. He guessed there must be a dozen or more other people there, all talking comfortably with one another. He liked just listening to the sound of their happy chatter. Some of the people had brought folding chairs with them, some sat on blankets they had brought, and others stood around.

Pretty soon one of the guitarists said, "One, two, three," and without any music to read the four of them began to play a peppy old tune. One person began clapping in time with the music and soon everyone was clapping their hands or tapping their toes as the music drew them together with its enthusiastic beat.

As soon as the song was over one of the men who was listening called out, "How about playing, *When the Saints Come Marching In*?" Joshua saw all the musicians look at each other, nod, and begin to play the request.

"I wonder if they know *Yankee Doodle Dandy*, Joshua said to his grandma and grandpa.

"I'm sure they'll be glad to play it if they know it. Just go ahead and ask when they finish this song," Grandma advised him.

But when that song ended someone else called out the name of another old song. And after that song, another song was suggested. Joshua began to think he'd never get to hear *Yankee Doodle Dandy*. Then he had an idea. As soon as the group finished playing he jumped to his feet and shouted, "Do you know *Yankee Doodle Dandy*?"

The little group of musicians looked at one another and nodded. But before the lead guitarist began to play he surprised Joshua by saying, "If you can sing it, we can play it."

Josh looked wide-eyed at his grandparents. He never thought that he might have to sing in front of these strangers. But he saw his grandparents nodding and smiling at him and looked around at the other people and saw them nodding and smiling, too. "Okay," he said, "I'll try, but I'm not sure I know all the words."

"If you have a problem, we'll help you along," the lead guitarist assured him. "We're not auditioning for *American Idol* here, we're just enjoying ourselves." And with that he began playing *Yankee Doodle Dandy,* singing softly to help Joshua get started. Before the first verse was over, Joshua was pleased to find himself singing as though he were alone in his own room. "This isn't as bad as I worried it would be," he thought as he kept singing.

As he sang the last note everyone there began clapping. Joshua felt his face getting warm and knew he must be blushing, but he could see how proud both of his grandparents looked as he returned to his seat. "Wow! Something else to tell my folks and my friends when I get home," he thought.

For probably another half hour the band played one old song after another. It was amazing how much music those people knew. But soon, just as people had begun arriving one by one or two by two, they began to drift away. Grandpa and Grandma looked at each other and then at Joshua and said, "It's time to be heading for home now."

On the way home Joshua could see why Grandpa had stopped to grab his flashlight before they left—the campground didn't have street lights. He hadn't noticed that before. There were a few lights here and there from outside lights on people's motor homes or campers, but sometimes the street was unlit for several homes in a row. It would have been easy to trip over something you didn't see in the road. So Grandpa had Grandma take hold of his arm and Joshua held her other hand as they all walked along with the flashlight illuminating the road a little bit ahead of them.

"This makes me think of a Bible verse. Can you guess which one?" Grandpa asked Grandma.

"I was just thinking of that," Grandma answered. "Psalm 119:105, 'Your Word is like a lamp for my feet and a light for my path.'"

"I don't get it," Joshua said. "How can the Bible be a lamp or a light?"

"You see how this flashlight is showing us things that could cause us to fall if we didn't see them?" Grandpa asked.

"Uh-huh."

"We can also shine it ahead of us and see where the next corner is so we know where to make a turn, can't we?"

"Uh-huh."

"The Bible tells us how to live the way God wants us to so we can recognize actions that might cause us to stumble in life and get hurt. It also can teach us how to look ahead and change the path we're taking if a different way to go would be better for us."

"Oh, I see. Sort of like a GPS, isn't it?"

"You've got the idea, alright," Grandpa said. "Very good."

"I see we're almost home," Grandma noticed. "The trip goes a lot faster when we don't stop to talk to people along the way, doesn't it?"

"Yeah, but it was nice to see your neighbors on the way there. Now when I'm at home and think of you I can picture some of your friends, too," Joshua told them. "Before we go in can we take time to see if I can find those stars that make up that picture in the sky? What did you call it?"

"A constellation," Grandpa replied. "Do you remember the two we looked at the other night?

"Right up there is the spread-out "W" that I remember you called The Queen, but I don't remember what her name was. And over there is the Big Dipper." Joshua proudly pointed to both of the constellations he had learned about earlier.

Grandma informed him that The Queen's name was Cassiopeia. And she also told him that if they wanted to have the old-time adventure of berry picking tomorrow they better be heading for showers and bed so they could be rested for their fun time in the morning. "If you've never been berry picking before I think you're in for a treat," she promised.

"Oh, boy!" Joshua sighed, "Another old-time adventure. I'm glad you had so many different things to do when you were growing up. No wonder you didn't have computers or TVs. You had too many fun things to keep you busy to even need them."

"Well, I've never thought of it that way before," Grandpa chuckled. "But it's an interesting way to end the day." And turning the flashlight on again so they could all see the way into the camper, he breathed a small prayer. "Thank You, Lord, for another day in your beautiful world, and for the blessing of another day with our grandson. May He continue to seek you with all his heart forever. Amen."

Chapter Six

Even with the blinds closed the sun filtering into the room woke Joshua. He could smell coffee, so he knew he wasn't the first one awake today. After stretching and yawning he sprang from bed and made tracks for the front room.

This time it was Grandma who was sitting in her chair alone with her Bible in front of her. She was underlining something on the page she held open.

"What do you do that for?" Josh questioned her.

"When I really like something I read I like to be able to find it more quickly. Underlining helps me do that."

"You and Grandpa really like God and the Bible, don't you?"

"You bet! Would you like me to tell you a couple of things about God while your grandfather is getting dressed?

"I remember He's our Creator, and Heavenly Father, and that He listens to us. And if He doesn't answer a prayer it's because He has something better for us. Is there more to learn than that?"

"If I were your teacher I'd give you an A for that answer. There is more to learn, though. Your grandpa and I are still enjoying learning. Maybe knowing that God is wise would be another thing you'd like to know."

"You mean He's smart?"

"Oh, He's that all right, but it's more than that. Let's pretend you did something wrong while you're here and Grandpa and I found out about it. After we talked to you about it, we might discipline you because of what you did. As much as we would want to discipline you correctly, we might somehow just not make the right decision. But when God disciplines a person He knows exactly the right way to discipline them. He doesn't make mistakes like people do.

"First, He forgives that person if they ask Him to. Always there is His forgiveness, but sometimes He also knows it is good for that person to receive discipline. The Bible tells us He disciplines those He loves."

"Why does He do that?"

"When God disciplines a person it's to give them an opportunity to learn. God is trying to help them change the way they are doing something so they can become better—more like His Son, Jesus."

"Oh. I see why you and Grandpa like to read about God so much," Joshua said, "but why don't other people? Mom and Dad don't read the Bible and they don't pray. And neither does anyone else I know. But after you've told me about Him this week I'd think everyone would want to be a friend of God and have Him be their friend."

Grandpa had walked into the room as Joshua was expressing himself. "We can tell you a little about why your mom is that way, since we're her parents," he explained. "She didn't grow up hearing about God because she was an adult before anyone told Grandma and me about becoming Christians and learning about God. So we didn't know how important it was. And now she's married and has you and your dad and a job and just seems too busy to make the time to go to church or to read the Bible.

"But I think she'd like to know the things you've been telling me."

"You know, Josh, we'd love to tell her, and at times we've tried, but she seems to think we're treating her like she's a kid. We don't want to hurt her feelings, so we just keep praying for God to reach her, and your dad, in some other way."

"I wish I knew how to tell them, but I don't know the things about God and the Bible like you do," Joshua said.

"You two have just given me an idea," Grandma interrupted excitedly. "When we take you home on Saturday we could tell your parents that you've asked us about God. And we could let them know that we've given you some Bible verses that tell about what we've talked about, so if they were interested they could read them, too."

"Oh, could you? Would you?" Joshua asked, obviously very pleased with the idea.

"While you and Grandpa find something to do this afternoon, I'll be glad to look up some verses and get them ready for you. Right now, if you two will excuse me, I thought I'd make some waffles for breakfast."

So while Grandma busied herself in the kitchen, Grandpa explained to Joshua a little bit about how the Bible is divided into two parts. "The first section is called the Old Testament. Everything in it happened before Jesus was born. And in the very first Old Testament book, Genesis, it tells about God creating the heavens and the earth. It also tells about God creating plants and trees; the sun, moon and stars; fish and birds and animals; and finally creating Adam and then Eve.

"Adam and Eve were the first of all the men and women who have ever been on earth," Grandpa continued. "And God placed them in a beautiful garden known as the Garden of Eden. He told them they could eat from any tree or plant in Eden, except from the tree of the knowledge of good and evil.

"But there was a snake in that garden and—wait a minute! Let me interrupt myself to ask you if you've ever heard of Satan."

"Isn't he someone who's wicked or mean or bad? I think he's in some stories, but I'm not sure if he's real, though."

"Oh, he's real alright. In fact, at one time he was an angel and lived in heaven. But he got very proud and wanted to be like God, so God threw him out of heaven and he ended up on earth."

"No kidding?"

"No kidding. Anyway, now that you know he's real, let me continue with the story about Adam and Eve. One day Satan disguised himself as a snake and he slithered over to Eve and began a conversation with her."

"Really? The snake could talk?"

"Yes, somehow Satan made a tempting voice come from that snake and it said to Eve, 'Has God said you shouldn't eat from every tree of the garden?'"

Joshua almost laughed because Grandpa sounded so funny trying to sound like he thought a snake would sound if it could talk, but Josh didn't want to interrupt the story.

Then Grandpa tried to make his voice sound as nearly like a woman's as he could so he could pretend he was Eve. "We can eat from any of the trees here in the Garden except from the tree of knowledge of good and evil. God told us not to eat from it or even touch it or we would die."

Returning to using his own voice he finished the story of how evil came into the world. "When the woman believed Satan's lie that the tree was good for food, and because it looked so good and she believed it when Satan told her that it would make her wise, she took one of the tree's fruits and ate part of it. She also gave the fruit to Adam and he ate some of it, too. And then they recognized that they had done wrong. They had disobeyed God by believing what Satan told them and following what he said, rather than believing God and doing what He told them to do."

Shaking his head Grandpa added sadly, "And because sin became part of their lives it then became part of their children's lives. And their children's children's lives, too. And sin has become part of the life of everyone ever since then."

"But that seems unfair!" Joshua said in a very upset tone of voice as he jumped up from the chair in which he had been sitting and listening. "I want to learn more about God and do what He wants me to. I really do. And that just doesn't seem fair to me. There should be a way to change it! You told me God is good! Why should I have to do wrong just because two people did wrong way, way back when the earth and the stars and everything was so new?"

Joshua was almost shouting, and he appeared to have tears in his eyes. He was shocked when he looked at his grandfather and grandmother and saw huge smiles on their faces.

"It's not funny!" he protested.

"Joshua, we're not laughing at you. We're smiling because what you're upset about has already been taken care of. That's what the New Testament, the second part of the Bible, is all about," Grandpa told him.

Immediately Joshua's whole attitude changed. "Really? Honestly? What happened?"

"God loved us so much that He already had a plan for what to do when Adam and Eve disobeyed Him. But I think Grandma's got those waffles ready and waiting for us. And I think I see blueberries peeking out of them. So why don't we just wait until later to talk about that plan."

"Okay, but I can hardly wait to learn about it," Joshua said. "I'm so glad to know God cared enough not to leave us without hope of being friends with Him. I've got a different question now, though—Can I try saying the prayer today?"

"That would be great." Grandpa said. And they all bowed their heads and closed their eyes as Joshua began, "Dear God, I haven't tried talking to you before so I'm not sure just how to do this, but thank you for these blueberry waffles. And for Grandma and Grandpa, and for that plan I just heard about that must be a good one. And thank you that I am learning more about you every day. I can hardly wait for Mom and Dad to learn, too. Amen."

Chapter Seven

Two small kittens lay sleeping under the shade of a large, old tree, while a beautiful Collie dog bounded across the driveway to greet Grandpa, Grandma and Joshua as they got out of their car at the berry farm. "How you doing, Laddie?" Grandpa greeted the dog as he patted his head. "You remember us after all these years, don't you?" And Laddie's tail wagged back and forth as he welcomed the three of them.

Grandpa walked over to the small shed. "Hi, Tom! Looks like business is good this spring. We'd like to pick three or four quarts of strawberries this morning. Where would you like us to begin?"

Joshua glanced ahead of them and noticed a few people out in the field, small boxes beside them, squatting down beside short green plants. One man carried his box heaped full of bright red berries as he limped to the little shed where Tom greeted customers and used a fishing tackle box for a cash register.

Motioning to his right, Tom said, "I'm just opening that section today. The other one is pretty well picked over, and I think you'll do better if you check this one out. If not, you just go right ahead and move over to where the other folks are finishing up."

"Thanks! Are you still allowing people to enjoy eating a few berries while they pick?"

"That's part of the pleasure," Tom replied. "I do believe if we didn't let folks do that a lot of people wouldn't even come to pick berries. And part of the enjoyment we get from growing these strawberries is seeing the pickers' smiles as they taste the berries fresh from the plants."

"We'll be back as soon as we've got all we want. See you then," Grandma said to Tom as they headed for the area he had pointed out to them.

Joshua watched Grandma and Grandpa each take a quart-size box and bend down to begin picking, and then he did the same. He had only put a few berries into his box when he remembered that he was allowed to eat a few, too. The next one he saw was a lovely bright red all over and the largest one he had seen. After he picked it he carefully separated it from its green stem and bit it in two. Sweet, pulpy juice filled his mouth and he felt a little bit dribble down his chin. "Oh, this is sooo good," he thought, and he quickly finished the first half and popped the rest of the berry into his mouth. "That was the best strawberry I ever tasted," he decided.

Then he noticed that Grandma and Grandpa were both ahead of him, picking more berries than he had. "I'd better stop eating and enjoying and start picking and saving, or they will be teasing me big time," he told himself. He bent down again and picked berries as fast as he could without ruining them by pinching them too hard to get them off the plant they were growing on.

It didn't take much time for bending to change into squatting and then back again to bending for all three of them. Either position for a very long time was difficult, but changing back and forth helped a lot. And each of them popped a strawberry in his or her mouth every now and then just because they were so nice and sweet and juicy.

It must have been almost an hour before they decided they had enough. It may have been that they had enough berries. Or it could have been that they had had enough of bending and squatting. Or possibly it was that they had enough strawberry juice on their fingers and faces and enough dirt on their clothes. But they had enough of whatever it was. So they returned to the small shed to pay Tom for the berries they had picked.

Tom measured the strawberries into a container and told them, "You've got a gallon of berries. That's a good morning's work. Looks like you've enjoyed tasting a few along the way, too. I'm glad to see that. A gallon of berries is four quarts. And the berries cost two dollars a quart, so that'll be eight dollars."

"They're well worth it, Tom. I think these are some of the best berries you've had yet," Grandpa said as he paid him. "They've always been delicious, but this year they're exceptionally good. Thanks so much. And have a blessed day."

"Thanks," Tom replied. "God has blessed us—with health and this business and good people like you as customers. It's always so nice to see you. May you be blessed until we see each other again next year."

"Thank you. But we might not wait that long. We're going to take our grandson home the day after tomorrow and we'll probably take a couple of these quarts to his parents," Grandpa told him.

"Great. Have a good trip. And I'll hope to see you again soon, then."

As the three of them climbed into the car for the return trip, Joshua spoke up. "Mom and Dad will love us bringing them some fresh strawberries. We don't have a farm near us where we can pick them. Did you pick those blueberries that you put in our waffles here, too?"

"No," Grandma told him, "we got them at a store, just like you have to. Blueberries like cooler weather than we have here so they don't grow well this far south. Grandpa and I didn't grow up picking blueberries but we both grew up picking wild raspberries and blackberries. They're not real pleasant to pick, either, because they grow on taller bushes that have small thorns on them. We both think that strawberries make your back ache more when it comes to picking, but blackberries and raspberries hurt your fingers more," Grandma told him. "But all of those berries are worth the little bit of hurting when it comes time to eat them."

"What are we going to do with all these berries that you aren't taking to Mom and Dad?"

"This afternoon we'll spend some time separating them from their stems, and tonight we're going to do our old-fashioned thing for today, besides picking them. We're going to make a freezer full of hand-cranked homemade strawberry ice cream."

"Is that as good as the ice cream we buy in a store?" quizzed Joshua.

"No," Grandpa replied.

"Then why make it?"

"Ha! Ha! Ha! Ha! Ha!" Grandpa laughed. "It isn't as good. It's better!"

"Oh, Grandpa, you're such a joker!" Joshua laughed in return. "I just love wondering what you're going to think of or do next."

Chapter Eight

By the time they were ready to eat supper, they all decided hot dogs cooked on sticks over a campfire sounded good. They warmed a can of pork and beans over the fire to go with them, opened a bag of vegetable chips, and had an at-home picnic ready in minutes.

As they were cleaning up Grandma had an idea that Grandpa and Joshua really liked. "How about the two of you playing a game of horseshoes while I mix up the ice cream recipe? Then both of you can crank the ice cream, and after that, while the ice cream hardens, the three of us can play another game of horseshoes."

"Yahoo!" Joshua responded.

"Sounds good to me, too," agreed Grandpa.

"I do believe you've gotten better at horseshoes while you've been here," Grandpa told Joshua as they threw their second round of the game. "You're lifting the horseshoes higher before you let go of them, and that helps them to go farther! Way to go!"

"Thanks, Grandpa! Guess I've been watching you and trying to do what I see you doing!"

"Now that's a real compliment. Hope I can live up to it. That's not a bad idea for life as well as horseshoes. You can read about a Bible hero and study his life and learn to avoid his mistakes and follow his good points. Then read about another one and do the same thing. You'll find that Jesus is really the best hero of all because He never made a mistake. Following what He taught and did is the best example you'll ever find. When we talk about the New Testament you'll learn about Him, because everything in the New Testament has to do with Him in one way or another."

"Why not talk about it now?" Joshua asked as he picked up his next horseshoe and prepared to toss it.

"We could, but I think it might be better if we don't have horseshoes and homemade ice cream on our minds at the same time as that. God's plan is so wonderful that it's good to be able to understand and appreciate it instead of just paying a little bit of attention to it.

"Besides, I think you may have tied the score with that horseshoe you just threw. I want to see if I can keep you from beating me before Grandma brings the ice cream mix out here for us to crank."

Grandpa tossed his last two horseshoes and he and Joshua were figuring their scores just as Grandma appeared on the scene with the large bowl of strawberry ice cream mixture she had prepared. "Joshua, would you mind opening the camper door and reaching inside and to the right. There's a bag of salt there for us to use in making the ice cream. If you'd bring it here we can get started."

"Salt? I never guessed that there's salt in ice cream," he said as he headed for the camper to get the bag.

"That's because there isn't salt in ice cream. This is a different kind of salt, the kind that you can put on your sidewalk and driveway if the weather is icy. You're going to be interested in seeing how it helps to make ice cream," Grandpa told him.

The ice cream churn was obviously old. The wood looked almost black in some places and quite worn in others. Some of the metal parts had rust on them, and the handle looked ready to be replaced. Grandpa said that only proved how much it had been used and appreciated. Grandma carefully poured the ice cream mixture she had made into the churn's inside metal container. Making sure that container was tightly capped, with the post of the churn paddle poking through the hole in its cover, Grandpa settled it in the middle of the old churn. Then he packed ice around it, added a fist full of salt, put in more ice, added some more salt, fastened the churn handle section to the paddle post, and settled it securely on the churn.

"Slow and steady is the way to go," advised Grandpa, after he had turned the handle a few times and then offered the job to Joshua.

"How long does it take?" Joshua asked as he took over.

"Sometimes it might be twenty minutes; other times it might be a little over half an hour. I thought you and I could trade off every now and then until it's done."

"I think I'd buy one of those electric ones," Joshua said, rolling his eyes.

"Oh, no." Grandpa differed. "Part of the pleasure of making ice cream is the joy of slowing down if you've had a busy day. It gives you time to think about what the best part of your day was, or decide what you might want to do tomorrow. Or you can just look around at other things. You know, like you did when we were canoeing."

As he cranked the ice cream churn for the next few minutes Joshua did just that. The first thing he noticed wasn't something he saw but something he heard. Someone nearby was playing horseshoes, just like he and Grandpa had been. He could tell by the *clank* and *thud* as first one horseshoe and then another smacked against the horseshoe post and then fell to the ground. Then he saw a colorful butterfly fluttering above a flowering bush. His eyes wandered from the hovering butterfly to the fluffy white clouds overhead. How white they looked against the darkening blue sky. Amazing! All those things had been there before, but he hadn't noticed even one of them. Maybe the idea of taking time to look around at God's creation was something he could try doing more often, he thought.

After a few minutes Grandpa walked over and added some more ice and salt to the churn. "Did you notice how some water was coming out of this little hole here near the top of the churn, and how the ice level is getting lower?" he asked Joshua. "That's from the salt melting the ice. Just like on an icy wintry sidewalk, the salt does its work. The ice melting in the churn allows the really cold water to completely surround the ice cream container. And as you or I turn the handle the paddle inside the ice cream mixture keeps stirring it so it will freeze evenly."

After each of them had cranked the churn a little while, and Grandma had begged them to let her have a turn, too, Joshua was cranking when he noticed something happening. "Uh-oh, I think something's going wrong with the freezer, Grandpa. It's getting harder and harder to turn."

"Oh, no, nothing's wrong with the churn. In fact, that's good news! It means the ice cream is very close to being ready to eat. Let me crank it a few times and see how much further it has to go," Grandpa said as Joshua stepped aside so his grandfather could take over again.

"My goodness, you've almost finished our evening's work here. Not very long now until we'll be enjoying in a very delicious way some of those berries we picked." And with that Grandpa gave the freezer handle a few final cranks and then removed the handle and crank from the churn.

Grandma moved in quickly and took the top off the ice cream container. "Oooh, doesn't this look good," she remarked eagerly, as Grandpa carefully removed the paddle with some difficulty from the frozen mixture. "Those little pieces of strawberry in with larger chunks of strawberry look just like I hoped they would. And I brought out some empty dishes that I put in the freezer earlier so our ice cream wouldn't melt so quickly," she added as she scooped out generous amounts of the frozen pink confection for each of them. Grandpa placed the ice cream container back into the churn so the ice cream would stay firm.

"Aaaah!" "Perfect!" "Delicious!" "Delectable!" "The best ever! "Outstanding!" "Superb!" "Scrump-dilly-ish-ous!" If you can think of the way you would describe the best ice cream you've ever tasted, it's the word you would have used if you could have been there to have a dish of that strawberry ice cream. You probably would have asked them if you could have a second dish, too; and maybe even more than that.

And it was as they were eating that simply perfect ice cream that Grandpa told Joshua the story he had been waiting to hear, a story that changed his life.

Chapter Nine

"Do you remember when I told you about Adam and Eve?" Grandpa began, as he ate the last bite of his second dish of that simply wonderful strawberry ice cream and set his dish and spoon aside.

"Yes, sir."

"Remember that God had given them a whole lot of good things to eat and only told them to avoid eating one thing?"

"Uh-huh. And they ate it anyway," Joshua said, glad that he could show his grandfather that he had been listening well earlier.

"Exactly! And that's really what sin is—choosing to do what we want to do rather than what God has told us to do. He has told us not to do certain things because He knows what can hurt us or someone else. And it makes Him sad to see us doing things that cause pain to ourselves or to other people. That's why He sets limits. It's like your earthly father putting a fence around your yard if a pit bull lives next door, and then telling you to be sure not to go outside that fence. You may not like being fenced in, but it's a lot better for you."

"I think I understand that Grandpa, but when I do wrong and feel bad about it didn't you say that keeps God from liking me?

"God will always like you, and even love you. Please never forget that. But when you do wrong, or we could say when you sin, that sin separates you from God."

"But that's what I don't want to happen. That's the plan you talked about that I want to know about."

"It's like this," Grandpa began. "Since sin separates people from God, God made a way for them to be close to Him again. His Son, Jesus, was willing to come to earth as a baby in human form. And when He grew up He began teaching people all around Him about God and what He was like and how God wanted them to live. He was very wise and caring, just like His Father God is. And Jesus did miracles, like taking a couple of fish and a few small loaves of bread, blessing and multiplying them, and then feeding thousands of people with them. And he healed people—like making a blind man see and a deaf man hear and a crippled person walk," Grandpa told Joshua.

"Cool!" Joshua said. "Everyone must have liked that! I'll bet He was the most popular guy around!"

"Not really. In fact, it became a problem, because the religious leaders didn't like Jesus being a better teacher than they were. They got jealous. He was good at using everyday things to help people understand more about God. He would ask questions they would have to think about, and then they would learn even more. The leaders got upset with Him. They wouldn't believe it when Jesus said God was His Father, and so they came up with a plan to kill Him."

"But God wouldn't let them do that, would He? I mean, you said God is strong. And you said He only does good things, so God wouldn't let them kill Jesus, would He?" Joshua protested.

"You know, I'm guessing that anyone living then who knew and followed Jesus must have thought just what you're saying. But what they didn't understand was that it was necessary for Jesus to die so sin wouldn't separate us from God the Father." Grandpa leaned forward as he continued to explain to Joshua about Jesus' death.

"For hundreds of years God had told His followers, the Jews, that for their sins to be forgiven they had to sacrifice a perfect animal. Only by the people shedding the blood of an animal that had nothing at all wrong with it could God accept their recognition of what they had done wrong and not hold them guilty for it. And then, as soon as they sinned again, they had to live with feeling guilty all over again until another animal was sacrificed."

"How could Jesus' dying help?"

"Remember that Jesus knew when He came to earth that He was going to change things," Grandpa continued. "By the life He lived He tried to teach people about God and show how good and powerful and patient and wise and loving God is. But He also knew that He was going to die, to be a substitute for the animal sacrifices people had been offering God for years for their sins. And that's why, when they planned to kill Jesus, He wasn't surprised."

After Grandpa paused to let Joshua think a moment, Grandma went on with the story. "The night he was captured by His enemies, He even prayed that God might not let it happen. But then He told His heavenly Father that what He wanted most of all was for His Father's will to be done. I think that must have pleased Father God very much. Jesus was much more concerned about making a way for people to be close to God again than He was about dying."

"Wow! That's awesome! But how did they kill Him? How did He die?"

Grandma really dreaded telling about what came next. She looked at Grandpa and nodded for him to go on with that part.

"After beating Him, spitting on Him, putting a crown of thorns on His head, and dressing Him in royal robes to make fun of Him, they made Jesus carry His own cross to a hill. Then, stripping Him to what back then amounted to his underwear, they nailed Him to the cross He had carried. And that's where He died," Grandpa said, completing the story of Jesus' crucifixion.

"How awful!" Joshua cried.

"Yes, it was," Grandpa agreed.

"But Joshua, there's a happy ending," Grandma told him, as she saw how sad he looked. "Jesus had told His disciples earlier that even though He was going to die, He would come to life again. They didn't think that could happen, so, like you, they felt terrible. And when a man who respected Jesus arranged for Jesus to be buried, they didn't even stay around for his burial. Only the disciple John, and Jesus' mother and a few other women had the courage to wait until he had died."

"Some friends they turned out to be," Joshua said.

"You're right. But you're also forgetting how loving God is," Grandma replied. "To go on with the story, there were guards set around the tomb Jesus was in, since some people were afraid His disciples might steal His body to make it look like He had come to life. That was on Friday night. But on Sunday morning there was an earthquake, and the stone that was closing the tomb was rolled away. And Jesus wasn't in the tomb because He had come back to life, just like He said He would. If you've heard of the resurrection, that's what it was. It was Jesus being raised from the dead!"

"Wow! What a happy ending! I'm so glad He didn't stay dead! But where is Jesus now?"

Grandpa took his turn again to answer Joshua's question. "He's in heaven, seated at the right hand of God the Father, where He's always praying for us."

"Awesome!" Joshua said, with a contented smile on his face. Then he tilted his head a little to one side and asked another question. "But how does that help me to be a friend with God? I don't get that part."

"God's plan was for Jesus to die for the sins of everyone. When a person recognizes they sometimes do wrong, or in other words, they sin, then they can ask Jesus to forgive them for sinning and to be their Savior. And if they have really meant that, they begin trying to live God's way instead of their own way. And that's the start of a wonderful friendship with God," Grandpa finished saying.

"It's that simple?"

"It sure is."

"Do I have to wait to go to church to do it?

"No, God lets people make up their mind about it any time and anywhere," Grandma said.

"How about here and now?" Joshua questioned excitedly.

"We'd be delighted and proud," Grandpa replied. And before Grandpa could even tell him what to do Joshua began to pray.

"God, I'm so sorry people treated your Son Jesus like they did. But I'm so glad He was willing to die for people and didn't change His mind. It's nice that He was willing to do Your will and not His own. I really thank You for Your plan. I'm glad I can let You know that I'm sorry when I do wrong. I know I've done wrong. Please forgive my sins. I really want to live like You want me to. Thank You, God. Amen."

As he opened his eyes Joshua was surprised to see Grandma wiping her eyes and he thought he saw tears in his grandpa's eyes, too. "Did I do it wrong?" he asked.

"No, no," Grandma told him. "Some tears are tears of joy, and that's what these are.

"I thought that ice cream was great," Grandpa said, "but this is even better. We couldn't have had a more perfect night. Uh-oh, Grandma, I think we never got around to that horseshoe game we were going to play with you."

"I'd forget about horseshoes any time if I could replace it with something like this," she said with obvious joy on her face.

And with a song in their hearts and joy on their faces they made sure the campfire was out, took the leftover ice cream and the dirty dishes into the camper, and all of them went to their beds with thankful, joyful hearts.

Chapter Ten

"Joshua, dear, it's time to wake up. This is your last day here and we didn't think you'd want to use any more of your time sleeping." It was Grandma's voice he heard, though at first it seemed to be part of a dream he was having. "Joshua, wake up! It's ten o'clock!"

"Ten o'clock! How did I sleep that long?" Joshua remarked as he sat straight up in bed. "I always wake up early. Give me a minute and I'll be right out." In a flash he was out of his pajamas, into his blue jeans and a Tshirt, and making the few moves needed to get to the kitchen with a hop, a skip, and a jump.

"Wow! I'll bet you've both finished reading in your Bibles and praying. Did you eat without me?"

"We've both had our coffee, but we decided we'd like to wait and have cold cereal with you since we're getting a rather late start on the day," Grandpa said as he tousled Joshua's already messy hair.

Each one prepared his own easy-to-fix breakfast and after a short prayer of thanks they all ate while they talked about what they would do on this last day together. "Have you ever played shuffleboard?" Grandpa asked Joshua. "And have you ever ridden on a bicycle built for two?" Grandma questioned.

"No, I haven't done either of those things. I can ride a bike, but I don't know if I could ride one that's made for two people."

With a hearty laugh Grandpa said that he'd be glad to ride with Joshua on a bicycle made for two people if Josh would like to give it a try. But Joshua reckoned that maybe he would rather like to play shuffleboard, since he had never gotten to try that, either.

"Oh, you don't have to decide between them," Grandma told him. "How would you like it if you and I played shuffleboard this morning while it's not too hot, since there's no shade over the shuffleboard courts? And this afternoon you and your Grandpa could ride one of those bikes around the shadier parts of the campground."

"Sounds good to me!" Joshua said as he carried his dishes to the sink. "Let me brush my teeth and comb my hair and I'll be ready to go."

It wasn't a very long walk to the shuffleboard courts. That was one of the blessings of living here. It wasn't a big campground, and nothing was so far away that you couldn't easily walk to get there. Before they began playing Grandma warned Joshua that she wasn't much better at this than she was at playing horseshoes, but at least she knew enough to explain how to play it. And no one else was there to see their mistakes, so they could laugh at themselves and with each other.

Joshua had to admit it was already almost too hot to play, but he did enjoy learning a few things about shuffleboard. In about half-an-hour they both decided the sun was just too warm, so they put away the equipment and headed for home. "The nice thing about quitting now is that neither of us had to be a loser," Joshua said with a laugh. "Wait until Grandpa asks who lost. We can both say, 'Not I."

You could probably say it was a lazy day. The sun blazed hot until evening, and even though Grandpa and Joshua had fun sharing their ride on a bicycle built for two, the heat kept them from wanting to spend much time doing even that.

"Seems to me if we're going to be doing anything active at all it better be more like swimming," Grandpa suggested, so the three of them changed into their swimsuits and went to the park's indoor pool. "A-a-a-h, at last," Grandpa sighed as he floated on his back in the clear, cool water. But the next thing he knew Joshua had taken a dive underneath him with the idea of surprising Grandma by splashing her from behind. Unfortunately, Grandpa was between them and got even more of a surprise than Grandma did. Soon the three of them were diving and splashing like a trio of porpoises.

Grandpa had once been on a swim team and Grandma had been a lifeguard, so they were quite at home in the water. "Can you do this?" one of them would challenge the other and Joshua, as they'd demonstrate a tuck or turn. And as soon as Joshua would try it, the other one would ask him if he knew a different swimming stroke or dive and show him how it was done. It was a wild, hilarious time as they romped together like porpoises until they were almost worn out.

"We'd better save a little energy for tonight," Grandma suggested, as she climbed from the pool and toweled herself off. Joshua and Grandpa appeared reluctant to follow her.

"What's going on tonight?" Joshua and Grandpa both asked.

"Oh, the campground is having a potluck supper."

"Pot luck? What kind of a meal is that? How can a pot have luck?" Joshua asked his Grandma, as he followed his Grandpa in climbing out of the pool.

"It's funny how you use words for years and know what they mean, but you don't think how they sound to people who have never heard them," Grandma said with a smile. "I don't know for sure, but I'm guessing the name for the meal must have started long ago when people got together in hard times to share their food and just encourage one another by being together. Anyway, a potluck is when each person cooks something and then everyone brings what they've made to a place big enough for them to put the pots, or dishes, or platters on a counter or table. Then everyone fills their plates with whatever they would like to eat from all that's been brought."

"Oh, I get it! They have luck if what they like is in a pot that someone brought," Joshua exclaimed. "Is that our old-timey thing for today?"

"Well, we thought it would be our one old-fashioned thing. But playing shuffleboard, and riding a bicycle built for two people, and swimming all were a part of growing up that we both got to enjoy. And tonight after the potluck they've planned to play charades, which was a game our generation played, too. We thought you'd like learning and playing it, too."

"That sounds like fun, but if you don't mind I'd rather we didn't stay for the charades, if it's okay with you," said Joshua.

"Have we worn you out today?"

"Oh, no! It's not that. It's just that I thought maybe we could play horseshoes since Grandma didn't get to last night. And I'd love to look at the Big Dipper and The Queen and the other stars again before I go home. And if there are lightning bugs tonight I hoped to catch a few to take with me."

"I'd choose Joshua's idea over charades any day," Grandpa said enthusiastically, as he slid into his sandals, held open the door for Grandma and Joshua, and they all headed for home.

"Sure smells good," Joshua commented a couple of hours later when they walked into the dining area of the clubhouse. As people began placing their dishes on the large table at one end of the room, he walked away from his grandparents and began looking at all the food that was there. Everything he saw looked as though it would be something he'd like to eat. How would he ever choose from among them all? Fried chicken, mashed potatoes, green beans, corn on the cob, ham, sweet potatoes, the taco salad Grandma had brought, a spaghetti casserole, macaroni and cheese, tossed salad, three-bean salad, slaw, enchiladas, deviled eggs, pickled beets, and more! And there was another table that was just for desserts! He turned away from the big table and went over to see whether the desserts looked as yummy as the things on the first table did.

He didn't think he'd ever seen so many temptations in one place. Angel food cake, chocolate cake, cherry pie, blueberry cheesecake, brownies, pound cake, apple pie, pecan pie, fresh fruit salad, a coconut pie, and all sorts of cookies. "Wow! What a feast!" he said as Grandpa walked up beside him.

"We thought you'd like coming to this," Grandpa told him as he smiled one of his warm smiles. "There's only one rule: you have to eat at least three things from the main table before you can head for desserts. And I'd suggest you don't eat so much you don't have room later for one last dish of that ice cream we made last night."

"No problem," Josh assured him, as they noticed Grandma motioning for them to join her at one of the tables where people would be sitting to eat. They had just reached her side when the person in charge of the gathering asked everyone to join together in singing, "God Bless America." A guitar strummed a chord and began playing as everyone began to sing. Joshua was surprised to see that the guy playing the guitar was the man who had been playing the night they took their friendship walk. It felt good to see someone he felt he sort of knew.

As soon as the hymn was over someone prayed for the meal and then the people headed for the two tables that were loaded with all the different things they had cooked and brought to share. One thing Joshua noticed was all the happy chatter, like when they had been together for the time of singing a few nights earlier. The sounds of laughter and sharing blended with the delightful aromas of the many different foods and created a mixture of pleasure that everyone seemed to be enjoying.

It's a good thing that Grandpa had told Joshua that they would be having some of their own wonderful homemade ice cream later that evening or he might have eaten way too much. He didn't know when he had wanted so much to eat at least a little bit of everything he saw. But he held back enough at the big table that he still had room for a piece of that chocolate cake with caramel icing. M-m-m-m good!

Saying their good-byes to the people they had shared a table with, they threw away the paper plates they had used, picked up the empty dish from the taco salad they had brought, and headed for home, their game of horseshoes, and one last dish of that scrump-dilly-ish-ous ice cream.

Chapter Eleven

The fireflies were just beginning to show up and show off their talents as Grandma, Grandpa and Joshua arrived home. "I want to try to catch a few lightning bugs before we play horseshoes," Joshua reminded himself and his grandparents, "that way I'll be sure not to forget."

"I'm guessing you wouldn't forget," Grandma said with a playful smile, "but I found a glass jar that I think should be just right for you. And Grandpa has punched some small holes in the lid. You can pull a little bit of grass to put in it, so they'll feel more at home, and then you'll be set to start catching them."

It didn't take long for Joshua to capture several of these small bugs that fascinated him with the way a part of each of them flashed off and on like a twinkling Christmas tree light. As he looked closely at one which he held in the palm of his hand, it lit up; and he marveled at its being able to do that. "How do you suppose that happens?" he asked his grandparents.

"I suppose some scientist could tell you that, but we sure don't know. We just thank God for all the different things he's put on this earth that we find pleasure in. And we also think of them as reminders of His wisdom and power and love," Grandpa answered him.

"How does a lightning bug make you think of God's love?" Joshua asked with surprise.

"You know, God could have made a black-and-white world, but he made it colorful. And He could have made a world without bugs, I'm sure, but He chose to use even something as small as this to make His creation even more interesting for us. That's a way He shows His love for us. It's quite different from showing His love by sending Christ to die for our sins, but it's still love."

"Just like your hugging Grandma shows her you love her, but so does chopping vegetables with her, or watching her favorite TV show with her?" Joshua inquired.

"Exactly! And just like your offering to play horseshoes tonight since I didn't get to last night shows love," Grandma suggested as she gave him a hug.

"Aw, Grandma!" Joshua grinned as he put the last lightning bug he planned to catch into his jar.

"And speaking of horseshoes, I have the game set up, so we can begin any time," Grandpa told them.

"How about right now," Joshua said as he sat the jar inside the back door and ran over to pick up one of the horseshoes.

One by one they took turns pitching as the *clanks* and *thuds* announced to the neighborhood that a game was going on. The day still hadn't cooled off a whole lot and one game was all it took for each of them to be quite willing to call it quits.

Just in case you wondered, Joshua came in second. Grandma and Grandpa didn't want you to know who won and who came in last, so we won't tell. But you can guess if you'd like to.

"Well, you've got your lightning bugs to take home, and we've played horseshoes. But I've forgotten what the other thing was that you wanted to do," Grandma told Joshua.

"I wanted to look at the Big Dipper and The Queen one more time. But I have a question about constellations first. Are there any more of those sky pictures like them, or are they the only ones?"

"Oh, there are many, many more constellations. Grandpa and I both used to know quite a few of them. But to be honest we've stopped looking for them and I've quite forgotten all of them but the Big Dipper and Cassiopeia. But there the Big Dipper is," Grandma said as she pointed to the stars that were the outline of that very large dipper in the sky.

"Before you come back again," Grandpa assured him, "we'll refresh our memories so we can show you some more constellations next time."

"Well, I see the Big Dipper now and I had already spotted The Queen, so I hope I'll remember them the next time I see a dark sky," said Joshua. 'You know, I felt sorry for you before, when I knew that when you were growing up you didn't have televisions or MP3 players or cell phones and all the things I've got. But I haven't missed those things while I've been here—or at least not much, anyway. And now I see that you had lots of good times without any of those things because you got to do all the fun things that we've done this week."

"But," he added thoughtfully, "lots of old people I see look so grouchy or sad, like they don't do any fun things or have any happy times. Why is that?"

"Well, lots of older people have problems with their health, or worries about not having enough money to pay bills, or are concerned about troubles their children or grandchildren have. And that can take a lot of joy out of life." Grandma said.

"But I know Grandpa has a heart problem, and you've got lots of allergies, Grandma, and you both have hearing problems, and I don't think you have lots of money, but you haven't gotten grumpy. Why have they?" he argued.

"You know those smiley faces that you can add when you're e-mailing your friends?" Grandpa queried.

Joshua nodded.

"Way back in the late 1970's or '80's when those were new, you sometimes saw a smiley face with the expression, "Smile, Jesus Loves You." We had asked Jesus into our lives at about that time, and we decided that would be a pretty good way to live. Since then, as we've read the Bible over and over, we've noticed that more than a thousand years before there were smiley faces God had made the suggestion to think about good things. Paul, who wrote a lot of what's in the New Testament, wrote a letter while he was in chains in a prison, telling people to think about the things that are good and worth praising and true and beautiful and that they respected. And of course when you think about those kinds of things they bring a smile to your face, because they are reminders of God's love."

Grandma spoke up, too. "Even way back when King David was alive in Old Testament times, he wrote a lot of psalms encouraging people to praise the Lord. He gave lots and lots of reasons to do that. He reminded them of God's greatness, and His goodness, of the beautiful and amazing things He had created, like the foods that grow in the fields; or the fact that God listens to them and that He loves them. And there are so many other things that God does for us, all of which should bring a smile to our faces if we think about them long at all. So we decided that 'Smile, God Loves You' would be a wonderful way for us to live our lives. Just another way of saying we would try to have an attitude of gratitude."

"Let me add one more thing," Grandpa said. "It's not always easy. Maybe you're not feeling well, or your best friend's just found out they're going to have to move away, or you need an expensive car repair. Then your mind wants to focus on the problem. That's when you have to ask God to help you control your thoughts. Have you ever been on a run-away horse?"

"Huh? Why are you asking me about horses when we're talking about this? I don't get it," Joshua asked with confusion.

"Give me a minute and I think you'll see the connection. But tell me, have you ever been on a run-away horse?"

"Yeah, one time. He was okay going away from the barn, but when I turned him to go back to the barn, he began galloping so fast I was totally freaked out."

"What did you do?"

"I pulled back on the reins as hard as I could but he still kept running. If I hadn't ducked when he was going back through the barn door, I would have really got hurt big time."

"But you did think to pull back on the reins. That was important. Since you weren't old enough to have a lot of strength, he didn't respond to you, but if you had been stronger, he would have stopped. When we find our minds running away and not obeying what we know is the best way for them to be going, we have to treat them like that runaway horse and stop them."

"But remember, Grandpa, I couldn't stop the horse. What if my mind keeps going?"

"That's where prayer and the Bible come in. You ask God to help you stop your mind. God is powerful, remember? And you also build up your spiritual muscles by memorizing verses that will help you rein in your mind. Together you and God can do it. That's the kind of thing Paul meant when he wrote, "I can do all things through Christ who gives me strength."

While Grandpa and Joshua were talking Grandma had quietly gone into the house and filled three small dishes with their ice cream left over from the night before. She brought them out and gave them each a dish as Joshua told his grandfather, "I'm really glad you could answer my questions about God and that you told me about Jesus. I hope my mom and dad and Mike and my other friends will want to learn about them, too. Do I know all I need to know now, or is that like the constellations—are there more things that I can learn?

"Would you believe that Grandma and I are still learning? That may sound like there must be more than you will ever want to know. But if you go home and find a good church you'll learn in fun ways, like when you learn a new song or play a Bible game. And you'll make other friends who want to learn, too. And as you discover what the Bible teaches about God's character and what He values, that will help you to live a life that's pleasing to God."

"And while we don't have a lot of your electronic things," Grandma spoke up, "we do have a computer and know how to email. And we do have a cell phone. So there are two ways that you can ask us questions if you need to, or if you just want to call and talk. And I know this is changing the subject, but would either of you like any more ice cream?"

With that Grandpa stood up, stretched, rubbed his stomach and said, "No, thank you. I don't think there's room in there for even one more bite, no matter how good it is."

"Me either, thanks," Joshua agreed. "Anyway, that will give the two of you a little ice cream to come back to tomorrow after you take me home."

"Before we go inside for the night, why don't we take a little time to thank God," Grandpa suggested.

"Sounds good to me," Joshua agreed.

"Me, too," Grandma said. And they took one another's hands, bowed their heads and closed their eyes.

Grandpa began: "How thankful we are, Lord, for the beauty of your creation and the love you shower on us. We marvel at things like lightning bugs, yet even more we stand in awe of how each thing you've put here on earth has a purpose. We thank you for giving us your written Word, the Bible, and teaching us so much through it about You and Your love and Your desires for our lives. How much You have blessed us, and we give You thanks for all that in Jesus' name. Amen.

Grandpa's *amen* was hardly out of his mouth when Joshua surprised his grandparents by adding a prayer of his own.

"Thank you, God, for all I'm learning about You. I am so happy You forgive my sins because You want me to be Your friend and want to be my

Friend too. How cool! Oh, and please, please help me be able to share all these awesome things with Mike and Mom and Dad so they can come to know about You, too. Amen"

Grandma felt she would like to talk to God, too, so she added her prayer to theirs. "Heavenly Father, my heart is overflowing with thanks for this time You have blessed us with while Joshua has been here this week. We are so thankful that he wants to know You better. Help him to find the right people to help him grow in Your ways. And may he always have a heart to love and serve and please You. Amen."

And so, with a beautiful, starry night above them, their tummies too full for even any more of that scrumptious ice cream, and hearts overflowing with thankfulness to God, they went inside and each of them had a night of pleasant dreams.

Chapter Twelve

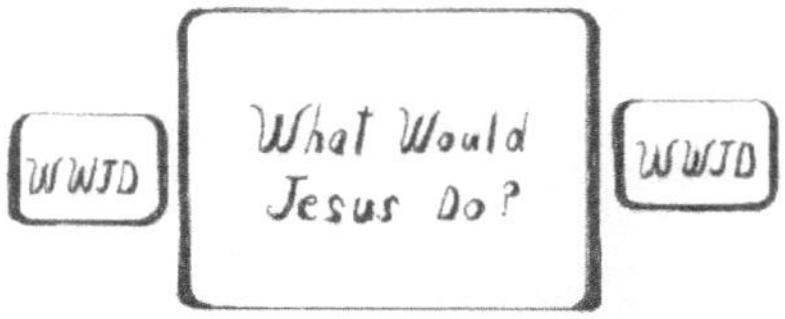

For the first time that week the sound of an alarm clock woke Joshua. "Today I go home," he thought, and he smiled as he pictured his arrival back home to hugs from his mom and dad. He could hardly wait to tell them about all he had seen and done and learned this week. And then he would jump on his bike and go see Mike and some of his other friends. He knew he could text them, but he wanted them to see his lightning bugs. They'd think the fireflies were as cool as he did.

He slid off the bed and out of his PJs and got dressed for the day. As he tiptoed out of the room he saw that Grandma and Grandpa were already reading their Bibles. "We just read an interesting verse in Isaiah," Grandpa told him, "and thought you might like to talk with us about it before we have breakfast. Would you?"

"Sure! What does it say?"

Grandpa began reading aloud, "The LORD says, 'My thoughts are not like your thoughts. Your ways are not like my ways. Just as the heavens are higher than the earth, so are my ways higher than your ways and my thoughts higher than your thoughts.'."

"That's it?"

"Yep, that's it."

Joshua thought a little bit and then said, "Well, I can understand the part about the heavens being higher than the earth, because we could see that real well on the nights we looked at the stars. And they look like they are real far from here. But I'm not so sure that I understand about the thoughts and ways part of what you read."

"What you mentioned about us looking at the stars is the kind of thing God was saying in that verse," Grandma encouraged him. "If you think of people here on earth and picture God thinking any thoughts about them, wouldn't you guess that what He thinks is much greater, or you could say higher, than anything people could come up with?"

"I guess so, because you told me the Bible says God is wise. And you also told me He's good and loving. And if He's like all that, His thoughts are better or greater or higher than how I think, that's for sure."

"Exactly. That would be true about the thoughts any person could think. God's thoughts would always be higher than theirs. And that's true about our ways, too. His ways are higher than people's ways, too."

"I don't think I get that part," Joshua admitted.

Grandpa was obviously listening to the conversation. With a finger pointed at himself and then at Grandma, he asked Joshua a question. "You think we're pretty great, don't you?"

"Uh-huh. I sure do."

"Do you think we're perfect?"

"No, maybe not perfect, but you're close to it," he answered fondly.

"You don't think we never make a mistake, or sin, do you?"

"No, as good as I think you both are I know everyone makes mistakes and sometimes does wrong, even you."

Grandpa pursued Joshua with one more question. "And does God make mistakes? Does He ever sin?"

"You told me that He could only do right, and He couldn't tell a lie or break a promise."

"Does that help you understand that His ways aren't the same as our ways are?"

"Yeah, now I get it," Joshua admitted.

"When you get home and have to make up your mind about some things and aren't sure what to do, maybe it will help you to ask yourself an old-time question, WWJD, which means What Would Jesus Do? You'll almost always notice that what you think He would do is a higher or better thing than many people would do. That will help you in making choices. And that's our Bible study for this morning. We had our prayer time before you got up, so let's go fix breakfast, eat, and hit the road, okay??

"Sounds good to me, though I'm still sort of full from last night. Would you believe it?"

They all agreed juice and toast was all the breakfast they wanted to have, so it didn't take long for them to fix it, eat it, and get ready to leave. Joshua had already packed most of his things, and only had to get his jar of lightning bugs, and gather a few things he had brought along to have in case he got bored. "Guess I didn't need those at all," he thought as a big grin spread across his face. *Boring!* was not a word that he had needed to use this week.

Singing, joking, and counting cars with out-of-state license plates helped three hours in the car pass quickly and soon Joshua's hometown lay just ahead.

"Don't forget we wanted to stop at a Christian bookstore before we go to their place, Honey," Grandma reminded Grandpa.

"Do you know where one is?" Grandpa asked Joshua.

"Oh, there's one at the mall we're just coming to. I've never been in it, but I've seen it. It's right beside the ice cream store. That's why I'm sure they've got one," he laughed.

"I'd suggest having an ice cream cone if I didn't know your mother's fixing lunch," Grandma said.

"Too soon for store-bought ice cream, anyway," Joshua offered. "After the strawberry ice cream we've had this week how can any other kind of ice cream taste really good again?"

"Now that's a compliment I'll remember for a long time, thank you!" Grandma said with a very broad smile as they entered the mall.

Joshua led them to the Christian bookstore and proudly ushered them in. He was surprised to see all the things that they sold. He had thought it would just have books, books, and more books. But there were pictures, toys, posters, lots of CD's and DVD's, a greeting card section, some T-shirts, games, and a bunch of other things. And of course there were also books, books and more books, which is the section of the store Joshua noticed his grandparents were heading toward.

He browsed around the different areas and then made his way to where they were busily comparing one book with another. "You're just in time," they greeted him. "We want to buy you a Bible of your own so you can read scriptures, too."

"Neat. Very cool. Thanks!"

After looking them over Joshua chose a Bible from the three different Bibles his grandparents had thought might interest him. They bought it and some thank you notes Grandma liked, and headed for the car.

It was a short drive from there to Joshua's home and his parents must have been watching for their arrival because the minute they pulled into the driveway the front door flew open and both his mom and dad rushed out to greet them.

Joshua threw his car door open and leaped out as soon as the car came to a stop. "Mom! Dad! I've missed you. I had a wonderful time, but it's great to be home. I've got so much to tell you! We picked strawberries and made ice cream. And we pitched horseshoes and went canoeing and did so many old-fashioned things. We saw lots of stars and . . ." and Joshua stopped for a moment in the middle of his sentence, almost like he had stopped in mid-air when they were in the canoe. "And the coolest thing happened," he began again, with a look of awe on his face. "I asked about the stars and Grandpa and Grandma told me about God creating them. And then later the more questions I asked about God the more Grandpa and Grandma told me and I ended up asking Jesus to forgive me and come into my heart. And He's there now and I want to learn more about Him and they got me a Bible, and. . . ."

"Whoa, slow down, son," his dad told him. "You've got lots of time to tell us all about your week. Let's take your things into the house first. Then we can hear more about things while we eat."

The first thing Joshua grabbed was his jar of lightning bugs. "Look what I've got! Do you know what they are?" he asked his parents.

"Lightning bugs!" both his parents answered eagerly. "I haven't seen fireflies for years," said his dad. "How great that you found some. I'd almost forgotten that they even exist. Guess I've been in the big city too long."

"And you said you picked strawberries," Joshua's mother said. "How nice that you could do that, too."

"We brought you some of them," Joshua told her excitedly.

"How would a strawberry pie sound?" his mother asked.

"I could help you; I've been helping Grandma and Grandpa cook! Haven't I?" Joshua looked to them expectantly.

"He's been a great helper in the kitchen," Grandma said.

"And in lots of other ways, too," Grandpa added. "We're going to miss him."

They all enjoyed their lunch while Joshua talked almost non-stop about all he had learned and how he'd decided that life way back when Grandma and Grandpa were kids wasn't so bad after all. And when they had all finished eating he jumped right up and began helping to take the dirty dishes off the table. "I learned how to be part of a team whether we were canoeing or cooking or cleaning up. And guess what! It's neat to work together—like a team—just like it is when Mike and my other friends and I play ball together."

"Sounds like maybe you did a little growing up this week," his dad observed.

"I'm also trying to learn how God would like me to live. Remembering to think about others before you think about yourself is part of that."

"Well, we'll certainly be interested in hearing more about what you learned," his mother said thoughtfully.

"Oh, that reminds me, since we talked with Joshua about God's character and about Christianity, we thought it might be helpful to you if we wrote down some of the verses that refer to those things. They might help you if he talks about them or has some more questions about them. Joshua has the verses printed off and stapled together in his suitcase," Grandma told her.

"Thanks for doing that. It may help. You know we haven't been going to church, and I'm not sure this will change our minds. But we won't discourage him if he wants to go. We just believe in letting him make up his own mind," Joshua's mom said.

"We can appreciate that. But of course not knowing what Christianity is about would have given him little reason to decide in its favor. We just appreciate the fact that he is so interested in things around him. If he asks questions and there aren't verses about what he's talking about on the list he has, we'd be glad to have you call and we'll help all we can."

"Okay, Mom. Thanks! We might do that."

"We hate to eat and run, but we know you have tickets for the three of you to go to that ball game tonight. Come to think of it, where did Joshua go? I want to be sure to give him a big good-bye hug before we leave. It's been such a joy to have him this week."

"That's good to hear. We wondered if he might almost be too much for you since you aren't used to having kids around anymore. I think the guys went outside so Dad and Joshua could see the GPS we bought yesterday. It will really be helpful when we get into parts of the city we're not familiar with, or when we take long trips," Joshua's mom said as she started toward the door so they could join the others.

It wasn't easy for Joshua to say good-bye, because he had had such a good time. At the same time, he still had so much he wanted to tell his mom and dad. And he wanted to go see Mike and his other friends and share with them about the exciting things he'd done and learned. They'd be amazed, like he was, to learn that life must have been fun even when there weren't all the great things they enjoyed playing with today. He hugged his grandpa and grandma and thanked them for his wonderful week. And he was a little surprised to find himself holding back tears, even though he felt so happy.

"Good-bye," he called as they got in their car. "I love you! Thanks for everything."

"Good-bye," they echoed. "We love you, too! We love all three of you. Be sure to keep in touch," they said, as they waved to Joshua and his dad and mom. And they fought back tears, too.

Grandpa started the engine and backed out of the driveway. Grandma reached her hand over and laid it gently on Grandpa's knee as they headed for home. "Good-bye's are so hard when it's someone you love so much. It really was a good week, though, don't you think?"

Grandpa reached down and squeezed her hand as he replied, "It was a wonderful week. Joshua's such a bright little boy with such a loving heart. And I'm so glad God gave us lots of opportunities to answer his questions about God and Jesus. I look forward to seeing what the Lord's going to do in his life."

"I've already started thinking about what we might want to do next summer when he gets to spend time with us," Grandma said. "Maybe we could take a trip some place, like to a state or national park, and see some of the wonderful things God has made—like waterfalls or geysers or redwood trees or a cave or two. God's made so many fantastically beautiful things. What would you think about enjoying some of them with Joshua? Wouldn't he make any trip even more special?"

Grandpa laughed a laugh of pure delight, thinking of all the possibilities they could choose among. What fun they would have checking out different ideas and then deciding which one could be next summer's adventure for the three of them.

As they continued their drive homeward they began thanking God for their wonderful week with Joshua and praying for God to bless him as he told his friends and his mom and dad about his old-fashioned fun and his newfound faith. Then, with hearts content because of the week just ending and dreams they were already starting to dream, they praised the Lord for the hope of more times for the three of them to laugh and love and learn together.

Part 3: I AM Statements

Because Jesus knew those who followed Him often had little education, He thoughtfully used a comparison (or symbol), which the rest of each "I AM" statement helped them understand.

I AM The Bread Of Life

Did you know that twice when Jesus was with His disciples He took very small amounts of food, prayed over them, and the little bit of food became enough to feed hundreds of people? Amazingly what began both times as just a few small fish and a little bit of bread became so much food that when leftovers were picked up there was even more food left than before Jesus accepted what people had given Him!

Bread is something most people eat a lot. If you have lots of money you can have lots of fancy selections and do all sorts of yummy things with it. Or if you're poor you can usually buy bread cheaply at a day-old-bread store. But because bread's available to rich and poor alike and fills a basic need it's definitely considered a necessity.

Jesus said "I AM the bread of life" because the more people who come to know Him by reading the Bible, praying, and spending time with other people who know Him, the more fully their deep spiritual hunger will be satisfied.

Then *they* would tell *even more* people! And eventually everyone would know Jesus! Wouldn't that be great? Exactly what He wants! And just think—He gave *us* the joy and privilege of being part of His wonderful plan!

(If you'd like to read and underline or highlight the "bread of life" verses in your Bible, they are: John 6:35, John 6:48 and John 6:51.)

I AM The Light Of The World

Genesis is the first book of the Bible. It's named that because *genesis* means beginnings and it tells about how God created everything. God only needs to speak and things happen! God said, "Let there be light" -- and there was light! The sun warmed the day. And the moon and stars were also created. Though it might seem like a big nightlight to some, the moon has power to control tides and many other things in nature. And stars are helpful navigational tools which also add beauty to the night sky. Many of their other benefits still lie unknown to us.

God also made a lovely garden, Eden, and created a man and woman, Adam and Eve, to care for it. The two of them had a close friendship with God. He told them they could eat from any tree in Eden except one. But a sneaky snake tempted Eve to eat fruit from that tree and she convinced Adam to eat some, too. Immediately they were sorry because they knew they had done the one thing God asked them not to. That was the first sin ever, and they owed God a big debt for ruining the perfect beginning He had given them in the garden of Eden. It affected them, the children they would have, and every person (including you and me) who has been born ever since then.

But here's a scripture that brings us wonderful news: "For the wages of sin is death, but the *free gift of God* is eternal life in Christ Jesus our Lord" (Romans 6:23 NAS). And Jesus promised His disciples, "I am the light of the world. Whoever follows me will not walk in darkness, but will have the light of life" (John 8:12 ESV).

Becoming a follower of Jesus means you recognize you have a sin debt that only God can pay for you. But all you need to do to receive that gift from God is to pray something like this: "Lord, I understand now that Jesus lived and died to pay my sin debt. How thankful I am! I choose today to follow the light of Jesus' life. Please help me live in a way that brings joy to You, me, and those around me. Amen"

Jesus wanted His followers to follow Him and become lights for the world so we, too, can spread the light of His great love. What a privilege, and responsibility that is. May all our lights shine brightly as we joyfully fulfill this honor He's given us!

I AM The Door And The Good Shepherd

Jesus talked to his followers about how He is the door and the good shepherd. When He did, He taught this as one lesson with two ideas He wanted people to understand. So we'll blend those two ideas into one story, too. It's not difficult to think of Jesus as a shepherd taking care of sheep, because we think of him as lovingly caring for everything and everyone He has created. And lots people have seen pictures of Jesus carrying a lamb. But to picture him as a door—that's harder, don't you think?

Jesus often talked about sheep because everyone in Israel, where He lived, was familiar with them. But different flocks of sheep had different kinds of care. Some city folks took their sheep to a nearby village where they could leave them in a public pen overnight. It didn't cost much because the people watching them were only watching them to make a little money. But thieves often tried to break in and take sheep since they knew those gatekeepers wouldn't put up a fight. They'd rather let the sheep be stolen since they weren't theirs anyway.

If you lived in the country, though, you made your pen from rocks you gathered from your *fields*. You stacked the rocks high enough for sheep not to jump over and left a space just big enough for you to lie across. *You became the door!* Once inside this barrier of rocks with a caring shepherd who knew them well enough to call them by name, the sheep would go to sleep. They knew *their* shepherd would keep them safe!

Can you see the lesson Jesus wanted us to learn from this story He told? Isn't it wonderful that Jesus loves us *that much! Wow!*

I AM The Resurrection And The Life

Resurrection's a big word, isn't it? And it's probably not a word you use much. But if you've planted a seed and later seen it sprout and bloom a flower or grow a vegetable, that's a good example of a resurrection. That seed you planted went into the ground, died, and then came to life in a larger, even more beautiful form.

When Jesus knew He would soon face death He told his disciples, "I am the resurrection and the life; he who believes in Me shall live even if he dies" (John 11:25 NAS). A few days later Jesus was crucified—that means hung on a cross to die - by people who had not believed the teachings He gave or appreciated the miracles He performed.

The law at that time only made it possible for Jesus' friends to put his body in a tomb after He died. But as soon as they could they returned to the tomb. When they arrived they were surprised the stone in front of the opening had been rolled away and Jesus' body was gone! Not only had Jesus left his grave clothes behind, the napkin which had been over his face was rolled up [some versions say folded up] in a place by itself. (John 20:6,7) That really made them happy!

Why? Because back then many people had servants. Servants washed their owners' feet, helped them dress, cooked the meals—actually they did anything and everything they were told to do. Some did it out of love and respect; others out of fear. But if the master had to leave a meal he would let the servants know not to clear his place by rolling up (or folding) his napkin and leaving it behind. It was a silent, visible message that he would soon return.

Are you thinking, "But Jesus lived *two thousand years ago* and I thought He always keeps his promises—why did He break that one?" It's a good question. The fact is we tend to look at time from our side and not from God's. Remember when we talked about beginnings in Genesis—when God made the world and Adam and Eve sinned? Just as God wasn't surprised by their sin and already had a remedy, He also knows there are people who still haven't accepted Jesus, but are going to someday. And He's lovingly giving them time.

If you have relatives or friends who still haven't asked Jesus into their lives, there's something you can do to help them. Begin to pray for them! You can write their names on sticky notes and put them here and there around you. Like inside your school locker. On your bathroom mirror. The refrigerator. Or inside your backpack. (Make sure no one minds, of course.) And every time you see one of the notes or one of those people, pray for them, And enjoy praying, waiting, and watching to see God changing their life for the better. Just like He's doing for you!

I AM The Way, The Truth, and the Life

Have you ever been in a car when the driver's getting directions from the voice guidance system and tries to argue with it? The owner/driver has never been to their destination, had looked at possible routes, but is now receiving contradictory directions. A final decision about which route to take needs to be made immediately! But which way should the driver go?

Thankfully, Jesus made sure His followers can avoid such uncertainty.

Before Jesus died He and His disciples had a meal together. As they ate He reminded them of the life they had lived together for almost three years. They had had both good times and difficult times together and were close friends, with Him as their teacher/leader. He told them He would be leaving to prepare a place for them and that they already knew how to get there. And He added, "I am the way, and the truth, and the life; no one comes to the Father *but through me*" John 14:6 (NAS).

Jesus didn't want them to feel like people today do if they're headed for a destination but can't get clear directions to arrive there. He told them (and us) that the way to be with Him is to follow the road His followers had walked with Him as friends. Lots of other ways to live will always be around to tempt us because there are many other ways to live. But to have the blessings Jesus offers in our lives here on earth and then to be with Him in heaven after life is over He made it clear: "No one comes to the Father *but through me*."

Aren't you thankful Jesus left you—everyone, really—with clear instructions on how to have a satisfying life *now and forever*? I'm sure Jesus hopes you feel even more desire to pray for people who don't know Him. Just think how happy you and they will be when you all get to heaven and get to thank Him for all He's done for you! You know, there's no reason we can't also thank Him every day each time we think of it. Think I'll start right now. How about you?

"I AM the true vine"

If someone asked you how long it would take to count to a billion could you answer them? Did you know that the average person in America lives to be about 79? And if they could somehow start counting one number a second from the moment they were born it would take their entire life to count to a billion!

Here's another astonishing statistic: Since Jesus' death billions and billions of people have become Christians! Remember what Jesus taught when He said He was the resurrection and the life? He said he would be like a seed you plant that dies but then brings new life. And that people who accept him and commit to follow him would find new life. He certainly proved it true, didn't He?

You've read Jesus' previous "I AM" statements. He shared one more. It's so important you don't want to miss it. He said, "I AM the true vine, and My Father is the vinedresser . . . you are the branches; he who abides in Me, and I in him, he bears much fruit; for apart from Me you can do nothing," (John 15:1,5b NAS).

Abide isn't a very familiar word; it simply means where you live. So if we want to "bear much fruit," for Jesus (which means have good spiritual results), we need to be sure we live as close to Jesus' example, and what He taught, as a branch is to a tree (or a grapevine).

Jesus knew tough times were ahead for his disciples. He was aware that sometimes they would have each other for comfort and help. But other times they would be beaten or stoned, shipwrecked, starving, and put in prison. And some would even die. Just for believing in Jesus.

It's comforting that scripture tells us that except for Judas all the men who were with Jesus when He made those "I AM" statements remained faithful to him. Part of the reason they did was because of who Jesus was and is and the promise of heaven where they will live forever. But they had another reason, too. They deeply desired to be good examples for those who might meet or hear or read about them.

Jesus taught, and with his disciples lived, in ways that have led billions and billions of people to become His followers! I hope you're one and that his "I AM" sayings, his other wonderful teachings, and the whole Bible will help you eagerly and joyfully always follow him closely.

Now may the God of hope
fill you with all joy and peace in believing
that you may abound in hope
by the power of the Holy Spirit.
(Romans 15:13 NAS)

Part 4: Poetry and Music

God delights in putting songs in people's hearts! He also gives people the ability to reflect, reason, and then rhyme! And if painting is their passion, it's because before they were even born God put parts (called cones and rods) in their eyes so they would know red from green, pink from purple, and straight from crooked.

When we use any of the gifts God has given us in a way that helps someone come to know Him better we bring Him great joy!

How could you use a gift God has given you to help others know Him? If none of the gifts written about above are yours, don't worry! That's only because there's not enough room to list all the gifts God's given everyone. But First Corinthians often focuses on love. If you read chapter 12, in verse 28, among the gifts, you'll see a small word, *helps*. Doesn't sound very important, does it? But all you need to do is ask where anyone would be if no one helped them—ever. Then put the idea of help together with a focus on love! What a powerful package!

If you look around you or just think a bit I'll bet you could make a list as long as your arm of ways you can help people. And as you pray about it God can demonstrate His love by helping you help more people than you ever imagined. Let's give it a try:

First let's start at home

In my bedroom ____

With laundry____

Other inside chores____

Outside jobs ____

School____

A neighbor____

A friend____

What a wonderful way to increase other people's joy! And yours! And to bring great delight to God by how well you demonstrate His love. And that's the best possible reason for anything we do.

God Loves Me S-o-o-o Much

Story One

God made my eyes
So I can see
A pretty flower
Or a bug or a bee.
God loves me s-o-o-o much!

God made my nose
And I can tell
A pizza or a cookie
By what I smell.
God loves me s-o-o-o much!

God made my ears
To help me hear
Loud and soft sounds,
Both far and near.
God loves me s-o-o-o much!

God made my hands
So I can touch
Family and friends I love so much.
God loves me s-o-o-o much!

God made my feet
To help me run,
Or climb a hill,
Or play in the sun.
God loves me s-o-o-o much!

God made my mouth
So I can say
Kind words to others
Every day.
God loves me s-o-o-o much!

God made my heart
So I can show
His love to others
That I know.
God loves me s-o-o-o much!

"God Made a Special World"

by Shirley McCoy

Story Two of the "God Loves Me S-o-o-o Much" series

God sure loves me!
And you know,
This whole world tells me so!
Do you know He loves you, too?
Check it out.
You'll find it's true!

Look above you in the sky—
See the clouds go floating by.
See a tree that gives you shade.
See a rainbow that God made.

Hear the raindrops hit the ground.
Hear the wind blow snow around.
Hear a dog bark at the moon.
Hear a songbird sing its tune.

Feel your grandpa's whiskery face.
Feel your grandma's warm embrace.
Feel the ocean lap your toes.
Feel a puppy's soft, wet nose.

Taste your favorite mac and cheese.
Taste some ice cream, if you please.
Taste a lemon's puckery punch.
Taste an apple's yummy crunch.

Smell the fragrance of a rose.
Smell the smell of just-washed clothes.
Smell a field of new-mown hay.
Smell the animals heading its way.

God made our whole world special so
His love for us will always show.
Look around you every day
And you'll see it's made that way.

"God's With Me Everywhere"

by Shirley McCoy

Story Three of the "God Loves Me S-o-o-o Much" series

I heard a birdie in a tree;
I think he sang his song for me.
It made me think of God above.
It made me think of His great love.

The Bible says this,
And that means it's true:
God's always with me
And He's always with you.

Though I can't see God
I do understand
He's right here with me
Wherever I am.

Since God's here
I'm never alone;
Don't need to text
Or call on a phone.

I know God's with me
When I'm feeling sad,
or when I feel sick—
or even if I'm mad.

If I get in trouble
I know God's still there.
I know He'll always be
Just as close as a prayer.

I talk to Him now 'cause
He's my best friend
And I know our friendship
Will never, ever end.

It makes me feel
Real good inside to pray
And tell God how I feel—
Sometimes lots of times a day!

It's like then He teaches me
That He really is real.
And that's the coolest feeling
I could ever, ever feel.

If you have no birdie
to sing a song for you,
Picture you in this story and
Just think what God could do.

The Bible says this,
And that means it's true:
God's always with me—
And He's always with you.

Would You Like To Give It A Try?

Have you ever thought you might like to write a few of your thoughts about something in the Bible? Not with lots of words, but just because you'd like to try expressing some of your thoughts or feelings. There's a style of writing called a didactic cinquain (pronounced: die DAK tik sin KANE) that you might enjoy giving a try - or lots and lots of tries! Here are the easy directions:

The first line is the title (or subject). There will only be a total of five lines so think what you want to write about—and what you might say about it in very few words on the next few lines.

On the second line write two words that describe the subject you chose.

On the third line you get to write a three-word phrase—or three gerunds (verbs ending in *ing*)—that describe your subject.

On the fourth line you write four words that describe feelings you (or others) have about the subject.

The fifth line is one word that repeats or is a synonym for the subject.

Here's a sample:

Jesus
My friend
Teaching, loving, healing
Light of my life
Forever

If you think I did that in two or three minutes, think again. I did lots of backspacing and starting over. But I really enjoyed the challenge (and the cinquain I created). I hope you'll like cinquains, too. You might even find a cinquain a unique way to text a loving sentiment to your grandparents or a far-away friend you're thinking about. You can practice on the lines below. Enjoy!

MAKING MELODY IN YOUR HEART

Music is amazing. It can move us to tears, inspire us to pray or praise the Lord, and prepare us to listen to the Lord speak through His Spirit and His Word.

Apostles Peter and Paul wrote about singing and praising the Lord while chained in jail cells. And while Paul was confined in Rome he wrote to the church at Ephesus, ." . . Sing and make music in your heart to the Lord, always giving thanks to God the Father for everything, in the name of our Lord Jesus Christ"(Ephesians 5:19-20 NIV).

With the distractions and uncertainties life presents to us today, our Lord still gifts us through Paul's music-themed message. The next time you feel "chained" by a situation, borrow a tune you know, or sing a tune of your own making and begin to thank God for everything that comes to mind. If nothing occurs to you, ask God to help you become more aware of your blessings and begin to make a list of them. Every day add three more things for which you're thankful, and in a week give singing and making music in your heart another try.

Isn't it awesome that God designed our obedience to His Word to become a blessing for us, His children — and that singing praise and thanks *to Him* lifts *our spirits* and brings deep joy to *our hearts.* When we find that happening it's a wonderful opportunity to thank our heavenly Father by praying something like, "May the songs in our hearts always bring you joy and glory," or "Thank you, Father, for the endless expressions of Your love."

Or if you know someone who doesn't know the Lord yet it's a time you can use to pray that God will help them come to know Him so they, too, can have a joyful song in their heart.

SATISFY US IN THE MORNING (Psalm 90:14) (NLT)

Score: Shirley McCoy

Part 5 - Hidden Treasures

HIDDEN TREASURES

Select verses from the Book of Psalms
which express some of the pleasures we can experience
in a satisfyingly warm and wonder-full relationship with our LORD

Preface

Meditation is an important element in revealing the depths of the riches in scripture. As you begin reading these verses, ask God to help you uncover the priceless insights which await

discovery. Slow down and focus on each verse; read it thoughtfully. Remember, meditation means contemplation, deliberation, and introspection.

The psalmists who penned these scriptures were skillful in conveying the beautiful relationship between God and the fantastically, complexly designed human beings who desired/desire to know, honor and more closely relate to Him. May your meditation on these verses become a relaxing/exciting experience on an ever more enjoyable walk with our wonderful Heavenly Father.

If you're new to things like this it may be helpful for you as you read a verse to notice what the psalmist is doing; what he anticipates the Lord doing, or what the Lord has already done that the psalmist is responding to; the interaction talking place between God and the writer-psalmist; and the facets of God's character and multiplicity of emotions which are expressed. Perhaps your reflections will bring to your mind situations taking place in your own life or the lives of others you know. Allow thanks, praise and/or petitions to flow freely at such times. (It's part of the hidden treasure.)

Before beginning, let's take a moment for prayer. Dear Father, tune our ears to hear you speaking from your holy Word. We're awed that you desire for us to have a closer relationship with you. Whether time becomes a tyrant and limits our precious interval with you, or we have the blessing of a day set apart to sit at your feet, we ask you to inspire and nourish our souls. May our meditation on your scriptures become a time of our delighting in you, and you reveling in our delight.

May all that we are, and all your Word and Spirit transform us to become, fulfill your purpose for each of us and bring you glory, honor, and praise. In Jesus' precious name, Amen.

Hidden Treasures Psalms

Psalm 5:3, "In the morning, O LORD, you hear my voice; in the morning I lay my requests before you and wait in expectation" (NIV).

Psalm 13:5–6, "But I trust in your unfailing love; my heart rejoices in your salvation. I will sing to the LORD, for he has been good to me" (NIV).

Psalm 16:11, "You make known to me the path of life; in your presence there is fullness of joy; at your right hand are pleasures forevermore" (ESV).

Psalm 19:14, "May the words of my mouth and the meditation of my heart be pleasing in your sight, O LORD, my Rock and my Redeemer" (NIV).

Psalm 28:7, "The LORD is my strength and my shield; my heart trusts in him, and I am helped. My heart leaps for joy and I will give thanks to him in song" (NIV).

Psalm 32:10b, ". . . the LORD's unfailing love surrounds the man who trusts in him" (NIV).

Psalm 34:5, "Those who look to him are radiant; their faces are never covered with shame" (NIV).

Psalm 63:1–4, "Oh, God, you are my God; earnestly I seek you: my soul thirsts for you; my flesh faints for you, in a dry and weary land where there is no water. So I have looked upon you in the sanctuary, beholding your power and glory. Because your steadfast love is better than life, my lips will praise you. So I will bless you as long as I live; in your name I will lift up my hands" (ESV).

Psalms 63:5–8, "My soul will be satisfied as with fat and rich food, and my mouth will praise you with joyful lips, when I remember you upon my bed, and meditate on you in the watches of the night; for you have been my help, and in the shadow of your wings I will sing for joy. My soul clings to you; your right hand upholds me" (ESV).

Psalm 73:23–26, "Nevertheless I am continually with thee; Thou hast taken ahold of my right hand. With Thy counsel Thou wilt guide me, and afterward receive me to glory. Whom have I in heaven but Thee? And besides Thee, I desire nothing on earth. My flesh and my heart may fail, but God is the strength of my heart and my portion forever" (NAS).

Psalm 86:1–12, "Incline your ear, O LORD, and answer me, for I am poor and needy. Preserve my life, for I am godly; save your servant, who trusts in you—you are my God. Be gracious to me, O Lord, for to you do I cry all the day. Gladden the soul of your servant, for to you, O Lord, I lift up my soul. For you, O Lord, are good and forgiving, abounding in steadfast love to all who call upon you. Give ear, O LORD, to my prayer; listen to my plea for grace. In the day of my trouble I call upon you, for you answer for you answer me. There is none like you among the gods, O Lord, nor are there any works like yours. All the nations you have made shall come and worship before you, O Lord, and shall glorify your name. For you are great and do wondrous things; you alone are God. Teach me your way, O LORD, that I may walk in your truth; unite my heart to fear your name. I give thanks to you, O LORD my God, with my whole heart, and I will glorify your name forever" (ESV).

Psalm 89:1–2, "I will sing of the LORD's great love forever; with my mouth I will make your faithfulness known through all generations. I will declare that your love stands firm forever, that you established your faithfulness in heaven itself" (NIV).

Psalm 89:14–17a, "Righteousness and justice are the foundation of your throne; love and faithfulness go before you. Blessed are those who have learned to acclaim you, who walk in the light of your presence, O LORD. They rejoice in your name all day long; they exult in your righteousness. For you are their glory and strength . . ." (NIV).

Psalm 90:14, "Oh satisfy us in the morning with Thy lovingkindness, that we may sing for joy and be glad all our days" (NAS).

Psalm 91:14–16 (God speaking to the psalmist-writer and us), "Because he holds fast to me in love, I will deliver him; I will protect him, because he knows my name. When he calls to me, I will answer him; I will be with him in trouble; I will rescue him and honor him. With long life I will satisfy him and show him my salvation" (ESV).

Psalm 92:4–5 "For you make me glad by your deeds, O Lord; I sing for joy at the works of your hands. How great are your works, O Lord, how profound your thoughts" (NIV)!

Psalm 94:18–19, "When I said, "My foot is slipping," your love, O Lord, supported me. When anxiety was great within me, your consolation brought joy to my soul" (NIV).

Psalm 97:11–12, "Light is shed upon the righteous and joy upon the upright in heart. Rejoice in the LORD, you who are righteous, and praise his holy name" (NIV).

Psalm 100:4–5, "Enter his gates with thanksgiving and his courts with praise! Give thanks to him; and bless his name. For the LORD is good; his steadfast love endures forever; and his faithfulness to all generations" (ESV).

Psalm 103:1–5, "Bless the LORD, O my soul, and all that is within me, bless his holy name! Bless the LORD, O my soul, and forget not all his benefits, who forgives all your iniquity; who heals all your diseases, who redeems your life from the pit, who crowns you with steadfast love and mercy, who satisfies you with good so your youth is renewed like the eagle's" (ESV).

Psalm 105:1–4, "O give thanks to the LORD; call upon his name; make known his deeds among the peoples! Sing to him, sing praises to him; tell of all his wondrous works! Glory in his holy name; let the hearts of those who seek the LORD rejoice! Seek the LORD and his strength; seek his presence continually" (ESV)!

Psalm 106:1–2, "Praise the LORD. Give thanks to the LORD, for he is good; his love endures forever. Who can proclaim the mighty acts of the LORD or fully declare his praise" (NIV)?

Psalm 119:49–50, " Remember your word to your servant, for you have given me hope. My comfort in my suffering is this: your promise preserves my life" (NIV).

Psalm 119:75–76, "I know, O LORD, that your laws are righteous, and in faithfulness you have afflicted me. May your unfailing love be my comfort, according to your promise to your servant" (NIV).

From Psalm 139 (NAS):

Verses 1–6, "O LORD, Thou hast searched me and known me. Thou dost know when I sit down and when I rise up; thou dost understand my thoughts from afar. Thou dost scrutinize my path and my lying down, and art intimately acquainted with all my ways. Even before there is a word on my tongue, behold, O LORD, thou dost know it all. Thou hast enclosed me behind and before, and laid Thy hand upon me. Such knowledge is too wonderful for me; it is too high, I can not attain to it.

Verses 7–12, "Where can I go from Thy Spirit? Or where can I flee from Thy presence? If I ascend to heaven, Thou art there; if I make my bed in Sheol, behold, Thou art there. If I take the wings of the dawn, if I dwell in the remotest part of the sea, even there Thy hand will lead me, and Thy right hand will lay hold of me. If I say, "Surely the darkness will overwhelm me, and the light around me will be night," even the darkness is not dark to Thee, and the night is as bright as the day. Darkness and light are alike to Thee."

Verses 13–14, "For Thou didst form my inward parts; Thou didst weave me in my mother's womb. I will give thanks to Thee, for I am fearfully and wonderfully made; wonderful are Thy works, and my soul knows it very well."

Verses 15–16, "My frame was not hidden from Thee, when I was made in secret, and skillfully wrought in the depths of the earth. Thine eyes have seen my unformed substance; and in Thy book they were all written the days that were ordained for me, when as yet there was not one of them."

Verses 17–18, "How precious also are Thy thoughts to me, O God! How vast is the sum of them! If I should count them, they would out-number the sand. When I awake, I am still with Thee."

Verses 23–24, "Search me, O God, and know my heart; try me and know my anxious thoughts; and see if there be any hurtful way in me, and lead me in the everlasting way."

Psalm 145 (NAS):

Verses 1–7, "I will extol Thee my God, O King; and I will bless Thy name forever and ever. Every day I will bless Thee, and I will praise Thy name forever and ever. Great is the LORD, and highly to be praised; and his greatness is unsearchable. One generation shall praise Thy works to another and shall declare Thy mighty acts. On the glorious splendor of Thy majesty, and on Thy wonderful works, I will meditate. And men shall speak of the power of Thine awesome acts; and I will tell of Thy greatness. They shall eagerly utter the memory of Thine abundant goodness, and shall shout joyfully of Thy righteousness.

Verses 8–13, "The LORD is gracious and merciful; slow to anger and great in loving kindness. The LORD is good to all, and His mercies are over all His works. All Thy works shall give thanks to Thee, O LORD, and Thy godly ones shall bless Thee. They shall speak of the glory of Thy kingdom and talk of Thy power; to make known to the sons of men Thy mighty acts, and the glory of the majesty of Thy kingdom. Thy kingdom is an everlasting kingdom, and Thy dominion endures throughout all generations."

Verses 14–16, "The LORD sustains all who fall, and raises up all who are bowed down. The eyes of all look to Thee, and Thou dost give them their food due time. Thou dost open Thy hand, and dost satisfy the desire of every living thing."

Verses 17–21, "The LORD is righteous in all His ways, and kind in all His deeds. The LORD is near to all who call upon Him, to all who call upon Him in truth. He will fulfill the desire of those who fear Him; He will also hear their cry and will save them. The LORD keeps all who love Him; but all the wicked, He will destroy. My mouth will speak the praise of the LORD; and all flesh will bless His holy name forever and forever."

Psalm 147:1, "Praise the LORD. How good it is to sing praises to our God, how pleasant and fitting to praise him" (NIV)!

Psalm 147:11, ". . . The LORD takes pleasure in those who fear him, and those who put their hope in His steadfast love" (ESV).

If you've appreciated the Hidden Treasure you've discovered here and wonder where to find more, reread these verses and you'll likely discover some precious gems you've missed. Beyond the verses cited, the Book of Psalms offers additional scripture passages for enriching your relationship with God. Whether you explore Psalms further on your own or God's Spirit urges you to delve elsewhere in His Word, may He become the satisfying, centering passion of your life.

Illustration Credits

Page(s)	Illustration
22	Timmy's Big Move by Benjamin Purcell and used with his permission.
26, 29, 129	The Best Red Tennies Ever; Here, Kitty, Kitty, and God's With Me Everywhere (God Loves Me So Much, Story Two) by Kelly Purcell and used with her permission.
30, 34, 40, 47, 55, 63, 70, 74, 80, 86, 93, 101	Sketches from Tell Me About God, Grandpa by Kay Forton, used with her permission.
127	God Loves Me So Much, Story One by Kathy Purcell and used with her permission.

www.ingramcontent.com/pod-product-compliance
Lightning Source LLC
LaVergne TN
LVHW081323060426
835511LV00011B/1830